# Contents

# Introduction

Getting a pleasing outcome is not just about hard work.

In the film "A Beautiful Mind" starring Russell Crowe, his character, John Nash, uses an economic algorithm which later became known as "Nash's Equilibrium" to decide which girl in a bar he and his friends have the best chance of seducing. He strategises that if he goes for the prettiest, he will encounter more competition, and if unsuccessful, an attempted switch of affections to her friend will be even less likely to achieve the desired result. He concludes that "ignoring the blonde" from the start should maximise not only his chances of success, but the chances of all of his friends as well.

Shallow as it is, this example highlights the significance of strategy when it comes to achieving success. Of course, you need to put the hard work into preparing for your examination. But you should also think carefully about which question you choose; you should practise how you approach different question types, consider which topics might come up, and pay careful attention to trigger words and phrases.

*This leads to the same point that has been made in previous years: that centres would be rewarded by spending more time preparing their candidates for different eventualities in terms of the wording of the exam question. - Unit 3 Examiner's Report, 2013*

Examiners are human, and with many scripts to mark, you will make their job easier and your chances of success much more likely if you pay careful heed to their tips and comments, instead of leaving them to search for your skill as a philosopher like a needle in a haystack. It is my hope that the tips in this little book will make your hard work obvious, and easy to credit.

I wish you the best of success in your efforts to be an A-grade student.

Laura Mears

# What is the difference between AS and A2 examinations?

The most obvious difference is the mark allocation. Whilst the two categories - A01 (knowledge and understanding) and A02 (evaluation) - have remained, there are now more marks allocated to the A02 section (part b):

## UNIT 3

|  | AS | A2 |
|---|---|---|
| **A01 (part a)** | *21 marks* | *18 marks* |
| **A02 (part b)** | *9 marks* | *12 marks* |

## UNIT 4

|  | AS | A2 |
|---|---|---|
| **A01 (part a)** | *35 marks* | *30 marks* |
| **A02 (part b)** | *15 marks* | *20 marks* |

Whilst you are now expected to fulfil all of the required A01 level descriptors for fewer marks, you also need to turn up the heat on your part b, with greater detail and more advanced reasoning. The pages that follow will make these distinctions clearer.

# How to analyse the specification

## UNIT 3 - DEVELOPMENTS (EDEXCEL 6RS03)

Unit 3 (Developments) has been designed to build on the knowledge, understanding and skills developed in Unit 1 (Foundations). The examination follows the same format, but it asks for an exploration of different arguments, concepts and issues. As with the AS, the Edexcel specification for Unit 3 is broad, with the intention of trying to reward knowledge and understanding of a number of debates and areas within a topic. In some sections, particular scholars are expected or suggested, and I have made this clear below.

Where this is not the case I have tried to suggest which philosophers may provide scope for a helpful discussion on the topic in question. The important thing to remember is that whether or not the specification mentions specific scholars, it is expected that your response with be rich in reference to the works of relevant scholars - both supporters of the theory and critics.

To be an A-grade scholar you need to:

- Have a clear grasp of what the specification asks for generally, for each part of the question. For example, a clear point of view for part (ii).

- Have a clear grasp of what the specification asks for specifically, for each topic area. For example, the concept of identity in Life after Death.

The pages that follow will lead you in a study of these two considerations - general and specific.

# UNIT 3 - DEVELOPMENTS (GENERAL)

Candidates have 1 hour and 45 minutes to answer **THREE QUESTIONS** from **AT LEAST TWO DIFFERENT** areas of study. Most centres teach material from Philosophy of Religion and Ethics, but either could be taught alongside New Testament, or one of the six major world religions. It is also possible to answer one question from each of three areas of study.

*The majority of candidates opt for two philosophy questions and one ethics question, with a minority opting for two ethics questions and one philosophy question. - Examiner's Report, 2010*

It needs to be stressed here that there are huge dangers in trying to bank on three or even four specific theories coming up. If I had written a book called how to get a B grade, it would include this method of question-gambling. As I write I currently have a sixth-form student texting me a number of questions about which topics to select, saying "Help, I am confused!" Here is my attempt to make this as clear as I can.

## *Philosophy of Religion Questions*

- Critiques of Religious Belief with **EITHER** Religious Experience **OR** the Ontological Argument

- Life after Death **OR** Religious Language

# Ethics questions

*It cannot be stressed firmly enough that centres and candidates cannot expect to achieve good results by second-guessing the paper and setting limitations on what they prepare.*

*Any of the ethical theories could appear as stand-alone questions, or with either/or choices, or could be linked with religion and morality. Furthermore, a stand-alone question on religion and morality is always possible, but can never be guaranteed. - Examiner's Report, 2011*

So bearing in mind there are **TWO** questions set on **FOUR** topics in the first section, if you want to have the option of completing two Ethics questions, you need to revise the following thoroughly.

- Religion **AND** Morality

- **AND AT LEAST TWO** from the following list: Deontology, Virtue Ethics and Natural Moral Law and Ethical Language **OR** Justice, Crime and Punishment "with objectivity, relativity and subjectivity".

For Unit 3, the specification indicates that the following skills and aptitudes are desirable:

- Knowledge and understanding of a range of key concepts and terminology within the topic area, expressed accurately and fluently, and written in a clear and concise manner.

- An appreciation of the background to a theory or issue, such as the historical or philosophical context.

- Specific and detailed knowledge of key thinkers, sources and critics within the area of study, including quotations and references to their teachings and texts, as well as appropriately deployed examples, to show understanding of the main issues they raise.

- An ability to relate debates to wider issues within religion, human experience and the wider world.

- A clearly expressed and reasoned point of view, reached through a critical evaluation of the views of scholars, sound evidence, reasoning and careful analysis.

*Each question is broken down into two parts, part (i) and part (ii)*

▶ **Part (i) AO1 - Knowledge and understanding**

In the first part of the question, which carries the most marks (18/30), you will need to fulfil the first four of the five bullet points above. Start with a concise introduction that sets out clearly where you are going:

*Examiner's Tip: Show in the introduction that the answer will follow the pattern of the question set in a structured way, and deal with the evidence.*

Your answer should be dense with terminology, scholarship, quotation and sound reasoning, with examples appropriately deployed to show a clear understanding of the main issue(s) raised in the topic or argument under consideration.

The mark scheme asks for ideas to be:

*... supported by a range of examples and evidence to show breadth and/or depth of understanding.*

This means you can choose to either look at a number of issues and arguments, or one in detail. But if you choose to do the latter, be careful to look at a number of contributors to that argument, rather than continually quoting from the same scholar.

The mark scheme also asks for the A grader to write:

*Concisely ... lucidly ...*

This means that your sentences should deal swiftly with large amounts of relevant detail.

Here is an example from the Life after Death topic:

*Plato, a dualist, taught that whereas the body will one day cease to exist, the soul as a non-contingent entity cannot die, but will go to the higher realm of true reality (the realm of the forms). This view seems to be backed up in Judaeo-Christian thinking; Scripture states; "But if Christ is in you, then even though your body is subject to death because of sin, the Spirit gives life because of righteousness." (Romans 8:10)*

This segment is concise because it contains a number of key terms and concepts, reference to a scholar, as well as an important text, and it moves lucidly (with agility and flow) from one idea to another.

You can further improve your writing by ensuring that one paragraph flows from another through the use of link words and phrases, such as:

- Yet ...

- In extension ...

- By contrast ...

- Perhaps a more successful argument/criticism is ...

- A further consideration ...

- Building on the work of ...

- Furthermore ...

As the specification does not usually ask for certain scholars to be studied as compulsory elements, the question will not make reference to particular thinkers. In the individual topic content summarised below, you will therefore come across the phrase **SUCH AS** which gives suggested, rather than compulsory scholars for study. You will not, therefore, be asked to "Analyse Anselm's version of the ontological argument" or "Compare and contrast the approaches of Hume and GE Moore, in the area of ethical language." Rather, the questions will be more general to the topic as a whole, beginning with trigger words from a list contained in the syllabus:

- Analyse

- Compare and contrast

- Differentiate

- Distinguish between

- Define

- Examine

- Explain

## Strengths and Weaknesses

A discussion of strengths and weaknesses will usually come in part (i), and it is necessary to include this, even if it is not explicitly asked for in the terms of the question. A good way to prepare for this is to draw up tables of strengths and weaknesses for each of the arguments or defences proposed. It is important to link as many strengths or weaknesses as you can, with a philosopher, preferably with a quotation. This gives much more weight to your well-reasoned points.

## The difference between "Examine" and "Evaluate"

This above list stops short of using the word "evaluate" because that is reserved for part (ii). However, examination of the arguments and their strengths and weaknesses is needed for part (i), (unless the question in part (ii) asks specifically about weaknesses, in which case, save these for that section). In part (i) you should distinguish between strong and weak approaches, and show developments and improvements to the argument in question, such as how the modern versions of the ontological argument have revived it.

For example, you can use phrases like the following:

- Possibly the strongest objection to the argument is ...

- Yet perhaps the most convincing criticism is ...

- A major improvement to the theory may have come in the shape of ...

Such phrases will hugely aid the coherence and lucidity of your essay, as it moves from part (i) to part (ii). However, keep focused on the question in part (i), and save your evaluation for part (ii).

### ▸ Part (ii) AO2 - Evaluation

This part now carries 12/30 marks, so without it, you can only achieve a C grade. I say this because a surprising amount of students max out on part (i), and save little time, thought or material for part (ii). These are often conscientious souls, who seem to think "at least the examiner will know I have revised well". This is terrible exam technique! A quick plan before beginning the question will ensure that, with a conscious awareness of the time, there will be sufficient material and effort deployed to gain the majority of those precious 12 marks.

Trigger words for part (ii) are:

- Assess

- Consider critically

- Criticise

- Discuss

- Evaluate

- Interpret

- Justify

- To what extent

- Why

Some of these trigger words are not very helpful: explaining "why" or "discussing" are not necessarily evaluative concepts. It is perhaps more helpful here to stress that part (ii) is all about showing that you have critically assessed the material presented, and from this exercise, you have constructed a developed and substantiated point of view. Although you should not sit on the fence here, you do not need to take an extreme position; either rejecting the argument outright, or accepting it entirely.

Here is an example of a middle-position conclusion:

### Question - "To what extent can we say that the ontological argument for the existence of God has failed?"

*Having looked at traditional and modern versions of the ontological argument, it is clear that the argument as a whole has failed to prove God's existence de dicto (by definition). However, in my opinion, this does not mean it has failed completely, as its original purpose was to rationally underpin already-existing "faith seeking understanding" (St Anselm). Actually, the argument has triumphed victoriously; its critics have been unable to show belief in God to be logically contradictory, and when combined with the evidential offerings of the cosmological argument, belief in a necessary being actually takes on huge philosophical significance.*

With some questions it may be appropriate to explore the implications of your conclusion for belief in God, other religions, society or the world as a whole. For example, in the Ethics topic "Justice, Law and Punishment", you may conclude that retributive punishment will have greater health benefits for victims, longer-term reformation for offenders, and hence less crowded prisons.

## A2 Philosophy of Religion

There is no additional advice for Philosophy of Religion essays, but applying the skills and aptitudes above, one might like to consider including:

- broad categories about the argument, for example, whether the theory is empirical or rational; a posteriori or a priori; and whether it uses deductive or inductive reasoning

- relating the debate to issues about God's existence: atheism, agnosticism, theism or deism, and the nature of God as omnipotent, omniscient, omnibenevolent, etc.

Candidates should be able to demonstrate knowledge and understanding of the following areas of study:

▸ **The argument from religious experience**

Candidates should be able to demonstrate knowledge and understanding of:

- some versions of the argument, and contributions from scholars such as CF Davis, B Davies, Flew, Hick, Swinburne, Vardy

- analysis of the meaning and types of religious experience, as they relate to the existence of God

- key ideas, such as the premises of such arguments and key concepts such as analogy, credulity and testimony

- understanding and evaluation of strengths and weaknesses, such as problems of interpretation, alternative explanations and notions about the probability of this argument.

## ▶ The ontological argument

Candidates should be able to demonstrate knowledge and understanding of:

- key terms, such as a priori, deductive reason and key concepts, such as definitions of God, necessary existence.

- knowledge of the premises of the argument, key stages in this type of reasoning, and any significant stages in its development

- some ontological arguments from key contributors, such as Anselm, Descartes, Malcolm, Penelhum, Plantinga

- key strengths and weaknesses of the arguments, drawing on contributions from critics such as Gaunilo, Kant, Russell, Hick, etc

- the need to assess the argument's validity, and whether it amounts to a proof.

## ▶ The non-existence of God and critiques of religious belief

Candidates should be able to demonstrate knowledge and understanding of:

- the key concepts and terms surrounding this issue, such as atheism, agnosticism, materialism, naturalism, scepticism and unbelief

- sociological and psychological stances from thinkers such as Durkheim, Marx and Freud; arguments about the existence of God and the problem of evil may be used here, provided the material is focused on the demands of the question

- evaluation of the strengths and weaknesses of the views, which leads to an informed opinion.

▶ **Life after death - reincarnation, rebirth, resurrection, immortality of the soul**

Candidates should be able to demonstrate knowledge and understanding of:

- the religious and historical contexts for these studies (rebirth/ Buddhism; reincarnation/Hinduism; resurrection and immortality of the soul/various theistic traditions); note: some, but not all of the above topics will be examined in any given year

- key terms and concepts, such as "identity", notion of "life after death" and the relationship between the mind and body

- the need to evaluate the strengths and weaknesses of evidence and reasons given for a belief, and some attention to key scholars and debates, including the use of language.

▶ **Religious language - analogy; language games; myth and symbol; verification and falsification debates**

Candidates should be able to demonstrate knowledge and understanding of:

- contexts of key terms, for example, a theological context to analogy and logical positivism with regard to verification

- key terms and concepts such as meaning, function, realism, and postmodernism

- contributions from key scholars such as Aquinas, Wittgenstein, Tillich, Ayer, Flew, etc

- the need to evaluate the strengths and weaknesses of evidence and reasons given for arguments; the need to weigh up philosophically the merits or otherwise of the viewpoint.

## ▸ Technical vocabulary

The Edexcel syllabus contains no glossary of terms, but the specification repeatedly refers to the need for "a range of technical vocabulary". It is best to prepare a list of terms, along with definitions and learn them thoroughly. As with AS, it is worth saying that the phrase "using a range of technical vocabulary" is deployed both for part (i) and part (ii), so this is a very time-efficient task; you get double the credit.

Such a list may include the following terms, but you need to add your own, as well as the definitions from your textbooks and notes:

- Agnosticism
- Analytic statement
- Analogy
- A priori
- Atheism
- Contingency

- De dicto

- Deductive reasoning

- Deism

- Dualism

- In re

- Materialism

- Monism

- Necessary existence

- Numinous

- Omnibenevolence

- Omnipotence

- Omniscience

- Physicalism

- Rationalism

- Reductio ad absurdum

- Reductionism

- Theism

- Transcendence

## A2 Ethics

There is no additional advice for Ethics essays, but applying the skills and aptitudes above, one might like to consider including:

- broad categories about the argument, for example, whether the theory is deontological or teleological; absolutist or relativist; objective or subjective

- relating the debate to issues about the nature and role of religion in issues of morality, law-making, social action and the media.

Candidates should be able to demonstrate knowledge and understanding of the following areas of study:

## ▸ Critiques of the relationship between religion and morality

Candidates should be able to demonstrate knowledge and understanding of:

- development of the material used at AS, for example, for the Euthyphro Dilemma, consider the implications for God's nature, the relationship between the omnipotent God and an external source of goodness, the problems raised by God as the ground of moral values, and/or what it means for God to be good

- the work of key scholars such as Freud and Nietzsche.

You may also refer to:

- material discussed by RA Sharpe (The Moral Case Against the Existence of God, SCM) and John Habgood (Varieties of Unbelief, DLT)

- case study material which exposes the problems of deriving morality from religion, conflicting religious moralities, and religious moral systems which may be counter-intuitive, absolutist or non-universalisable

- one or more forms of the moral argument, but you "should not spend too long unpacking these arguments".

▶ **Deontology, natural moral law, virtue ethics**

Candidates should be able to demonstrate knowledge and understanding of:

- the philosophical, religious and cultural foundations of these theories (consider when they were developed, as well as how they sit in modern-day thinking)

- the key features of these approaches (absolute, relative, teleological and deontological principles); an evaluation of the efficacy of these theories for ethical decision making

- contributions of key scholars such as Kant, WD Ross, Aquinas, Hoose, Aristotle, and MacIntyre

- key strengths and weaknesses of the arguments, and evaluative conclusions drawn from these.

▶ **Meaning and definition of ethical terms with reference to "is-ought" debates about "good"; emotivism**

Candidates should be able to demonstrate knowledge and understanding of:

- the naturalistic fallacy - associated scholarship such as that of Hume and GE Moore; solutions to the problem, including intuitionism and non-naturalistic approaches to ethics

- other considerations about the use of the term "good" as functional, descriptive, realist or anti-realist

- the background to emotivism within philosophy of language, including the contributions of key scholars, such as AJ Ayer and the logical positivist school; evaluation of the role and effectiveness of emotivism

- an evaluation of these ideas about religious language, based on analysis of their relative strengths and weaknesses; drawing on ethical theories by way of illustration and comparison.

▸ **Objectivity, relativism, subjectivism**

Candidates should be able to demonstrate knowledge and understanding of:

- the above concepts generally, and in relation to specified ethical theories (note: do not repeat material between questions!)

- technical terms relevant to these approaches, for example, a discussion of ultimate moral truth vs feeling-based morality; source of moral truth; cultural relativism; absolutism, ethical pluralism

- evaluation of the strengths and weaknesses of these approaches, and of case studies as they relate to these concepts (and not pure narrative).

▸ **Justice, law and punishment**

Candidates should be able to demonstrate knowledge and understanding of:

- connections between the three ideas, for example how punishment might connect with the goal of bringing about justice

- any legitimate theories and material - religious or otherwise - relating to these three concepts; choose ones which offer "scope for debate and academic content".

Your answer may also benefit from:

- stating clearly which approaches you consider to be most helpful in approaching these issues, and what sort of society you would see emerging as a result of your findings.

▸ **Technical vocabulary**

As with Philosophy of Religion, I have included a suggested list, but you may need to add to it, as well as the definitions gathered from your textbooks and notes.

- Absolute

- Anti-realism

- Categorical imperative

- Consequentialist

- Deontological

- Ethical pluralism

- Eudaimonia

- Meta-ethics

- Non-naturalism

- Normative ethics

- Objective

- Proportionalism

- Realism

- Relative

- Retributive justice

- Secularism

- Subjective

- Teleological

- Virtue ethics

# UNIT 4 IMPLICATIONS (EDEXCEL 6RS04)

Candidates have 1 hour and 15 minutes to answer **ONE QUESTION** from their selected area of study. This question will be based around an extract from a particular reading, so you must be familiar with, and adept at analysing, all of the readings thoroughly.

*It must be noted that there is no predictable pattern in the choice of selected texts, however, over the lifetime of the specification all the three texts will be used. - Examiner's Report, June 2012*

The question will be structured in two parts, with 30/50 for A01 (knowledge and understanding) and 20/50 for A02 (evaluation). Be careful to time yourself wisely, leaving adequate time for each part.

*Some candidates spent too much time on part (b) in spite of the mark allocation. - Examiner's Report, June 2013*

The questions never vary, and nor do the expectations of what is required. Below is the question, along with the aptitudes and skills needed for each part.

## *Examine the argument and/or interpretation in the passage. (30)*

- "Proficient use" of key concepts and terminology within the topic area, written in a dense, detailed, fluent, well-structured and coherent style. To gain the highest grade, your use of technical language needs to be "crystal clear".

- "Comprehensive understanding" of the points made, and the beliefs held in the extract, along with "critical evaluation" of this point of view.

- "Clear and critical analysis" of these points and beliefs. This will include reference to alternative approaches to the view expressed in the extract.

- Application of relevant thinking taken from other readings in Unit 4, as well as material from Units 1-3.

▶ **Structuring part (a)**

The examiner's reports set out three ways to do this. You could:

1. Give a detailed exposition of the passage, that is, going through it line by line, expounding the meaning and significance of each key phrase. The danger here, however, is that the response becomes merely a narrative account of one section, which does not recognise the wider context of the passage.

2. To counter this, you could present an overview of the reading as a whole, picking up on the key ideas as they appear in the extract. The danger with this method however, is that you reach insufficient depth on the significant ideas of the passage.

3. Perhaps the best method then, is to follow a structure which places the extract in its context within the reading, before honing in on the significant points made within the passage. You could follow this paragraph structure:

    i.    As an introduction, set out the context and background of the reading from which the extract has been taken, including reference to author, historical context if significant (what was going on philosophically/culturally/politically), and what is at stake in this debate, for example, the logical right to call oneself an atheist.

ii.  Picking two or three ideas in depth, or four or five in less depth, work through the meaning and significance of key phrases in the extract (these can be highlighted when you read it through). Link each key phrase with scholarship, argument and ideas you have come across in other Unit 4 readings and Units 1-3 (this is important, as this paper is known as "synoptic", which means it should mesh philosophical ideas from different parts of the course).

The beauty of this structure is that it **FOCUSES** your response on the extract, whilst placing the passage in its **WIDER CONTEXT**.

*Do you agree with the idea(s) expressed? Justify your point of view and discuss its implications for understanding religion and human experience. (20)*

You need to include:

- a "statement of the student's own stance", which draws on scholarship, reasoning, religious terminology, evidence and argument

- a thorough exploration of the wider implications of the opinions in the passage, as well as your conclusions about their validity.

By "wider implications", the specification is referring to:

- the impact on and for **RELIGION**: If these views and conclusions were widely held, how would that affect individuals and groups within religion, and what would their impact be?

- the impact on and for **HUMAN EXPERIENCE**: If these views and conclusions were widely held, how would that affect individuals and groups in the secular world, and what would their impact be?

*It is important that these demands (do you agree?; point of view; religious implications and wider implications) are addressed in an explicit manner rather than implicitly. - Examiner's Comment*

### ▶ Structuring part (b)

The above comment means that you must make it clear that you are giving a point of view as to whether you agree or disagree with the arguments given in the passage, as well as reasons for that opinion. You should then go on to examine the implications of your view. Hence this seems to be a reasonable structure to follow:

1. Start by stating clearly whether you agree or disagree with the opinions expressed in the extract, and if you disagree, state what your opinion is. Next, give clear philosophical reasons for this conclusion; both why you have selected the opinion you have reached, and why you have rejected alternative views. Be careful here not to repeat what you have already stated in part (i). Rather, evaluate the arguments for and against, drawing on scholarship and related ideas to justify your opinion. This may take 2-4 paragraphs.

2. Look at the implications of your point of view, for religion. Ask yourself, for example, which religions would be affected by these conclusions (monotheistic? polytheistic? all?) and what those effects would be, for example, do you think if your view was universalised, religion would be strengthened? Altered? Die out altogether? What approach to the scriptures does your opinion endorse (voice of authority? Guide for life? Erroneous fiction?)?

3. Next look at the wider implications of your point of view, for example, in the areas of politics, ethics, the family and community. Would rejection or acceptance of an idea affect other related ideas and systems, for example, if religious experience is rejected, then what of other apparent supernatural events or beliefs? If moral objectivity is rejected, then what might bind communities in unity?

## Question 1 - Philosophy of Religion

There is no additional, specific, guidance on what sort of discussion is expected for each reading/topic area, but I think that a very sensible way to begin analysis of each reading is to draw up a list of vocabulary used in the extract. From this, you can then build a detailed translation of the main points made in the reading, and begin to decipher the "code".

- **READING 1** - "God-talk is evidently nonsense" - AJ Ayer in B Davies (editor) Philosophy of Religion: a guide and anthology (OUP, 2000) pp 143-146 © Philosophy of Religion - a guide and anthology, AJ Ayer, Dover Publications Inc.

- **READING 2** - P Donovan, Can we know God by experience? in B Davies (editor) - Philosophy of Religion: a Guide and Anthology

(Oxford University Press, 2000) pp 370-381.

- **READING 3** - M Westphal, The emergence of modern philosophy of religion in P Quinn and C Taliaferro (editors) - A Companion to Philosophy of Religion (Blackwell, 1999) pp 111-117.

## Question 2 - Ethics

See the guidance for how to proceed with revision for the first Philosophy of Religion reading above.

- **READING 1** - Method and moral theory - D Jamieson , Method and Moral Theory in P Singer (editor) - A Companion to Ethics (Blackwell, 2001) pp 476-486.

- **READING 2** - Personal relationships - H LaFollette, Personal Relationships in P Singer (editor) - A Companion to Ethics (Blackwell, 2001) pp 327-332.

- **READING 3** - Modern moral philosophy - J Schneewind, Modern Moral Philosophy in P Singer (editor) - A Companion to Ethics (Blackwell, 2001) pp 147-156.

# How to analyse past exam questions

## UNIT 3 DEVELOPMENTS (EDEXCEL 6RS03)

*The highest credit invariably is given to those candidates who are prepared to respond to the questions set, rather than writing a generic essay which does not directly fit the question asked. - Examiner's Report, 2011*

Exam board regulations mean I am unable to reproduce the exact wording of past questions, but I have summarised them for you in the grids that follow.

# PHILOSOPHY OF RELIGION

## *Critiques of religious belief*

|                                        | 2010 | 2011 | 2012 | 2013 |
|----------------------------------------|------|------|------|------|
| **Key ideas of two critiques**         |      |      | *i*  |      |
| **Evidence and reasons for atheism**   |      |      |      | *i*  |
| **No question**                        | *x*  | *x*  |      |      |
| **Existence of God**                   |      |      | *ii* |      |
| **Evidence and reasons against atheism** |    |      |      | *ii* |

*With considerably more candidates preferring to answer the question on the Ontological Argument or Argument from Religious Experience, this was a less popular question. - Examiner's Report, 2012*

It would be tempting to completely ignore this topic, but that is not the mindset of the A grader. She thinks: "Everyone else will concentrate on the obvious topics, so I will take some time on this hugely interesting area, and gain the upper hand."

> **Part (i) Analysis**

**Key ideas of two critiques (2012)**

There are two ways to approach this question; most students would choose two scholars, such as Durkheim, Dawkins, Marx or Freud, and work through a number of significant features of each. Linking your accounts with supporting and opposing scholars (the question says "examine" which means "look at critically"), as well as prominent examples, will make this a strong answer.

However, the examiner's report praised an approach that identified the word "critiques" in the first instance, with movements, rather than individuals. This enabled them to compare and contrast, for example the views of Jung and Freud within the psychological critique, as well as scholars within the sociological stable. What a good idea!

Note: The specification also indicates that you could utilise the problem of evil as a critique, but I would advise against this; it risks becoming too similar to Unit 1, and examiners said that candidates who made this choice often struggled with part b.

**Evidence and reasons for atheism (2013)**

Don't be put off by the use of the word "atheism" rather than the phrase "critiques of belief in God". This is still asking for analysis of the views of the main thinkers - Marx, Durkheim, Freud and Dawkins being the most popular. Lucid use of examples would be a good way to consider the evidence, and with this in mind, the problem of evil and suffering could be used wisely.

- ▸ **Part (ii) Analysis**

### Existence of God ("There is no God" - relating to one critique) (2012)

If you had taken the second approach in part (i) - described above - you are in a good position now to utilise the views of more than one scholar to build up the case that there is no God, as well as showing clearly the weaknesses in their points of view. Try to use the phrase "there is no God" a number of times, throughout your answer to show you are relating your evaluation back to the question. You can use this phrase even when you are arguing to the contrary, for example: "The challenges from Wittgenstein question our ability to say with any meaningful certainty: 'There is no God'." Make sure that your conclusion is specific; do you agree, disagree or partially agree?

### Evidence and reasons against atheism (2013)

Make sure you save your responses to the main critiques for evaluation in part (ii), but don't forget to explore more than one point of view, weighing up whether the ideas of key scholars stand up to scrutiny.

## Religious experience

|  | June 2010 | June 2011 | June 2012 | June 2013 |
|---|---|---|---|---|
| **Evidence and reasons to support belief in God** |  |  |  | *i* |
| **Essential ideas/Key principles** |  | *i* | *i* |  |
| **Existence of God** | *ii (a)* | *ii (b)* |  | *ii (c)* |
| **Strengths and weaknesses** | *i* |  | *ii* |  |

*(a) "probable" (b) "trustworthy" (c) "not conclusive"*

▸ **Part (i) Analysis**

**Strengths and weaknesses (2010, 2012)**

Perhaps the most tempting approach to a question on religious experience is to spend a significant amount of time churning through different types of religious experience as classified by two or three different scholars, for example, Swinburne's five categories and William James's four characteristics. However, such an approach is not the A grader's style. He recognises that this approach is boring, descriptive and irrelevant to the question.

The A grader instead lets the strengths and weaknesses guide his structure. He considers concepts such as the argument's inductive nature, the availability of a posteriori evidence, and the variety of religious experience as strengthening the argument. These are linked with prominent scholars and specific classifications, examples and key ideas, in order to expound why they add strength to the argument. By looking at a number of strengths with proficient use of terminology and argument, the A grader constructs a case for why the strengths of the argument might point to the existence of God. He then does the same for the weaknesses, drawing on such aspects as the subjective nature of religious experiences, and linking that key weakness with criticisms from scholars such as Dawkins.

**Essential ideas/Key principles (2011, 2012)**

A very important distinction to make with these questions, one that is easy to miss, is whether they ask generally about religious experience, or the argument from religious experience:

*A good response to this question typically opened with a reference to the argument from religious experience rather than to features of religious experience. - Examiner's Report 2011*

Listing different types or examples of religious experience is therefore not the way to engage with such as question.

*When the argument was the focus of the question, candidates were able to engage with the demands of the question, using premises and types of argument such as the inductive or cumulative arguments, and the contributions of Swinburne and Alston.*

*Ensure that you do not spend too long on types, descriptions or technical terms for religious experience, but proceed to the argument. - Examiner's Report, 2012*

Examiners are looking for a wide range of relevant evidence, useful scholarship and excellent breadth of knowledge and understanding debated with a fluent use of religious language. It is good to focus on key ideas and concepts such as Swinburne's principles of credulity and testimony; a priori/a posteriori and real/non-real experiences; neuro-science/psychology and James' typology/cumulative argument/ conversions. Material from a range of studies on religious experience, such as the Alistair Hardy Centre or Persinger's Helmet, can be used to strengthen or challenge the claims on which an argument is based.

Be cautious, however, about expanding criticisms in part (i), as for both of these questions, this discussion is better suited to part (ii).

The examiners welcome use of good examples, as well as cross-fertilisation from the anthology (Unit 4) although if you do this, you must make sure that you accurately summarise these scholars' views; some of the 2011 candidates suggested that Donovan was wholly in favour of the argument from religious experience, which is not the case.

**Evidence and reasons to support belief in God (2013)**

The question was broad enough to include both types of religious experience, and arguments from religious experience, so a whole range of material could be presented here, from experients, such as St Paul and Teresa of Avila, to scholars such as Buber and Peter Donovan, as well as the more obvious William James, Swinburne's principles of credulity and testimony and the cumulative argument.

### ▸ Part (ii) Analysis

### Existence of God ("probable" 2010; "trustworthy" 2011; "not conclusive" 2013)

It is important when discussing whether the existence of God is probable, that you include a discussion of the philosophical difference between probability and proof. A good grasp of the distinction between a posteriori and a priori arguments will help you to expand this discussion philosophically, as will an appreciation of subjectivity and objectivity - consider for whom the existence of God is made probable - the experient? The Church? The community as a whole?

*For a very effective approach, target the wording of the question from the first sentence and link everything you say with that wording. - Examiner's Report 2012*

You need to focus on "trustworthiness" if asked, and not just write about strengths and weaknesses. Some exploration of what it means to be trustworthy would be good here; foundational for faith or just legitimate as a way of strengthening already-existing faith?

You may like to consider here the vicious circle and conflicting claims arguments of Peter Vardy, or the scepticism of Dawkins and Persinger. Are there any arguments or types of experience that are more trustworthy than others, or are they all as untrustworthy as each other? Exploring the many ways you can utilise the terms of the question will be a great help in structuring a relevant response.

### Strengths (more convincing than) weaknesses (2012)

You could use a "straw man" type structure here; that is, where you build up a case through philosophical argument, then show why you disagree with it ("knock it down"). Some good ideas from the examiner reports included using the principles of testimony and credulity, Peter Donovan's article in the philosophy anthology (Unit 4), as well as relevant ideas about intuition and the self-authenticating claims of religious experience.

## Ontological argument

|                                                    | 2010 | 2011  | 2012 | 2013  |
|----------------------------------------------------|------|-------|------|-------|
| **Key terms/Essential ideas/Distinctive features** | *i*  |       | *i*  | *i (a)* |
| **Arguments**                                      |      | *i (b)* |      |       |
| **Strengths and weaknesses**                       |      | *ii*  | *ii* |       |
| **Argument is "obviously incorrect"**              | *ii* |       |      | *ii*  |

*(a) "a priori", (b) "for atheist"*

▸ **Part (i) Analysis**

**Key terms/Essential ideas/Distinctive features (2010; 2012; 2013 "a priori")**

An A-grade response to a question on the ontological argument will move beyond Anselm and Descartes to consider the more modern contributions of Plantinga and Malcolm. Yet it is really important for these question-types that you structure the content of your answer around the phrase used in the question, and not around a pre-prepared list of contributors and versions. Key features may include its a priori, deductive nature; God's essence (Descartes); and God's necessary existence. For the 2013 question, examiners praised the stronger answers for their "unrelenting focus" on the phrase "a priori".

Pitfall to avoid:

- showing up ignorance in chronology: examiners in 2013 were appalled that some candidates seemed to imply that Anselm was in some kind of direct debate with Hume, or Kant being overly attentive to Dawkins and Gasking at the expense of other critics.

## Arguments ("attempts to prove to the atheist that God exists" 2011)

*The heart of this question ... was in how far the candidate made the link with atheism. - Examiner's Report.*

It is important that these links are clear and explicit, and tackled head-on, from the start. The interesting debate here is whether each contributor was writing for the atheist at all; Anselm claims not to, then calls him "the Fool", meaning he has made a logical error. Descartes seems to agree; with his location of God's existence in his very essence he suggests that if you understand what is meant by divinity, then you will conclude automatically that He exists. Yet a decent amount of paper space must be given over to Malcolm and Plantinga, and here is a challenge: in 2011, "few candidates appeared to really understand these scholars' arguments". (Examiner's Report) Do you?

## ▸ Part (ii) Analysis

## "Obviously incorrect" (as an argument) 2010; "a priori proof provides no information" 2013

*The best answers were those who showed understanding of a priori, deductive reasoning and analysed how the outcome is not a logical consequence of the definition of God. - Examiner's Report, 2012*

For the 2010 question, a discussion of what the word "incorrect" might entail, eg in a realist or anti-realist sense, was an approach singled out for praise by examiners. For both of these questions, you should come to a clear conclusion about whether you agree, disagree or partially agree, giving full justification for your view, as well as your rejection of alternative views.

Pitfall to avoid:

- Writing a "strengths and weaknesses"-type answer, and tacking reference to the question on at the end.

**Strengths and weaknesses (2011; 2012)**

I recommend you discuss at least three critiques in depth here: Gaunilo, Aquinas, Hume, Kant and even Dawkins and Gasking are all up for grabs (always try to include at least one modern contributor). Even though Unit 4 is the explicitly "synoptic paper", you are invited by the examiner to pull in appropriate material from other areas of the course, for example, one example of good practice in the Examiner's Report (2011) makes links between the atheism/critiques of religious belief option on this paper, and the weaknesses of the ontological argument.

Pitfall to avoid:

- A simple statement of strengths and weaknesses, with little consideration of which may be more convincing.

# Life after death

|  | 2010 | 2011 | 2012 | 2013 |
|---|---|---|---|---|
| **Key concepts** |  | *i (two)* | *i (two)* | *i (two)* |
| **Compare and contrast** | *i (two)* |  |  |  |
| **Strengths and weaknesses** |  |  | *ii* |  |
| **Credibility of belief** | *ii* | *ii* |  | *ii* |

▸ **Part (i) Analysis**

**Key concepts (of two accounts) 2011; 2012; 2013**

The most popular accounts seem to be reincarnation and resurrection of the body, a choice which lends itself to a discussion of the "key concepts" of monism and dualism. If you choose to look at rebirth and reincarnation, you need to be adept at using the relative terminology, and expressing the nuances between these two Eastern theories, with reference to scholarship. Immortality of the soul is a topic which lends itself to some very detailed scholarly debate and examples from antiquity as well as the modern day. Singled out for praise in 2013 were "some excellent candidates who managed cleverly to weave more than two concepts into their responses, ie bringing immortality of the soul into reincarnation".

Scholars mentioned most frequently seem to be Plato, Descartes, Kant, Ryle and Hick, so perhaps you should include some less popular contributors, without ignoring these stalwarts. In all of your discussion, bear in mind that the question asks for the philosophical features that underpin belief in life after death, so stay focused on these instead of rattling through versions.

*The strongest responses included biblical references and quotations to discuss resurrection of the body, for example, Job 19:26, Daniel 12:2 and Ezekiel 37, as well as philosophical approaches to resurrection. - Examiner's Report, 2011*

Pitfalls to avoid:

- Unclear use of examples, eg about heaven and hell.

- Confusion in explaining certain concepts and views, notably Replica Theory and the views of Ryle.

- Giving purely narrative examples of resurrection accounts, near-death experiences (NDEs), or evidence of reincarnation.

- Referring only to the resurrection of Jesus, but not to the wider concept of the resurrection of the body.

- Writing a compare and contrast essay when asked for analysis of key concepts.

- Giving quantitative or evaluative bias to one account of life after death over another, particularly when looking at the views of different religions; your feelings or agenda shouldn't come into an academic debate.

### Compare and contrast (two accounts) 2010

There are many interesting ways to structure a question like this. In my opinion, one of the most "academic" is to structure your paragraphs around comparisons of certain elements, such as monism/dualism;

evidence; rational arguments. However, grouping the different elements from your selected two beliefs into similarities and differences is another excellent way to proceed.

Pitfalls to avoid:

- Comparing "unbelief" (hard materialism) with a belief that there was a life after death. This steals the thunder from part (ii), and does not do what is asked in the question.

- Using NDEs as an account of life after death; these should be referred to concisely as examples, and not taken as a belief about life after death.

### ▸ Part (ii) Analysis

### Credibility of belief (2010; 2011; 2013)

Try to give equal consideration to the view that life after death is and is not credible, highlighting the most convincing reasons for each point of view. It is important to keep these reasons academically and philosophically rigorous, and not resort to feelings or anecdote. Keep your reasoning scholarly; reference to Hume and Dawkins, and to Hick's replica and eschatological verification theories are all highlighted in the reports as good practice.

### Strengths and weaknesses (2012)

The question asks for strengths and weaknesses of arguments for life after death, so you are not restricted to a discussion of the two approaches you have analysed in part (i). You need to be familiar with the big questions surrounding these arguments, for example, the popularity of materialism; the moral arguments in a culturally relative world; the meaningfulness of God-talk. Are there responses to these prominent issues?

## Religious language

|  | 2010 | 2011 | 2012 | 2013 |
|---|---|---|---|---|
| **Compare and contrast/ Contributions** | i (two) | i (two) | | |
| **Meaningless or not** | ii | | i | i/ii |
| **Use not meaning** | | | ii | |
| **Importance ("indispens-able")** | | ii | | |

▸ **Part (i) Analysis**

**Compare and contrast (2011)**

When choosing which two types to compare and contrast, you may wish to bear the following points from the examiner's reports in mind:

- Some dealt with the via negativa to good effect, and excellent use was made particularly of material on myth and symbol.

- Candidates who chose verification and falsification were generally more adept at comparing and contrasting, but this was also the most popular choice, and it also paid quite nicely to save these two for part (ii).

**Contributions (of two) 2010**

The strongest answers to this question largely came from those who chose analogy (reference to Aquinas), and language games (with reference to Wittgenstein).

Pitfalls to avoid:

- Confusion over analogy, eg citing Paley's watch or Jesus' parables as examples.

- Confusion over the distinction between myth and symbol.

- Wasting time explaining the background to the religious language debate.

**Meaningless or not (2012, 2013)**

For the 2012 question, it is the preserve of the A grader to be au fait with quotations from prominent scholars, so to this end, she would have identified Wittgenstein as the source of the phrase used in the question; "Of what we cannot speak we must remain silent." Once identified, she will interact with the reasoning and background to the thinking within the quote, particularly, logical positivism, verification and falsification and language games. However the latter area could have been intelligently squirrelled away for part (ii). You might be tempted to choose two topic areas such as myth, analogy and symbol, but these might restrict your discussion of the meaning of the quotation. An excellent way to proceed, highlighted by examiners, is to choose discussion of realist and anti-realist language as your two types, which then allows you to address the question in more depth. Good practice highlighted in the 2013 report includes; using religious language examples, addressing verification and falsification in depth, awareness of the Logical Positivist movement, bringing in scholars such as Braithwaite, showing an awareness of the early and later Wittgenstein; use of Hick's eschatological verification, Hare's "bliks" and Mitchell's partisan and the stranger.

Pitfalls to avoid:

- Ignoring a quotation or stipulation used in a question, and just ploughing on generically about religious language.

- Misreading the question as meaningful for (i) and meaningless for (ii), and therefore getting material the wrong way around!

## ▸ Part (ii) Analysis

### Use not meaning 2012/Meaningless or not 2013

Keep in mind that this is an evaluation question, and hence it does not call for narrative of other types of religious language, although scholarly debate within these can be utilised, for example, Wittgenstein's discussion of language games, and arguments for and against Ayer's approach to language. The key to unlocking the 2012 question has to be a grasp of the difference between use and meaning, followed by building up and/or knocking down a case on behalf of each focus. For 2013, verification and falsification may feature prominently, but you could also discuss the strengths and weaknesses of your chosen theories of religious language, as long as you follow the wording of the question. This question follows a for/against structure, but there is also room for questioning whether the meaninglessness or otherwise is really the central issue; is "use" a more important quality of language?

*Use of a few, well-chosen and relevant quotations lifts your essay into a higher level. Make sure you have one or two good quotations for each topic you write about in the exam. - Examiner's Report, 2010*

**Importance ("indispensable" 2011)**

Make sure you show understanding of the term "indispensable", and make full use of it here. You may like to consider which aspects of religious belief rely particularly on religious language, for example, morality (Unit 3) or experience (Units 3 & 4), but keep your evaluation critical, scholarly and dense in terminology throughout.

Pitfall to avoid:

- Ignoring the question, such as outlining strengths and weaknesses of types of religious language, or focusing on whether religious language is meaningless.

# ETHICS

## Religion and morality

|                      | 2010  | 2011 | 2012  | 2013   |
|----------------------|-------|------|-------|--------|
| **Important concepts** | i (a) |      | i (a) |        |
| **Success or weakness** | ii    |      | ii    | ii (b) |
| **No questions**     |       | x    |       |        |

*(a) two critiques, (b) i virtue ethics*

▸ **Part (i) Analysis**

**Important concepts**

The first thing to be clear about is the difference between a critique of religion and a critique of the link between religion and morality. In order to do the latter, you must keep your focus on the reasons given to undermine the link. The Euthyphro Dilemma, the writings of Richard Dawkins, Marx and Freud could all be useful here, but only if they are examined rather than outlined by use of examples and clarification by reference to related concepts and contributors.

*Use of biblical examples to support critiques of religious morality are more helpful than attempting to construct imaginary or hypothetical scenarios. - Examiner's Report, 2010*

If you are asked to examine one or two critiques, make it clear from the start which particular ones you are examining. If you are asked to consider only one critique you need to explore the topic in depth, although this could include reference to other linked scholars and critiques. Make sure you save new and relevant material for example on responses, for part (ii).

## ▶ Part (ii) Analysis

### Success or weakness

For a question on the overall success or weakness of one critique (2010), you need to keep your focus on an evaluation of the material outlined in part (i), and not digress into a generalised weighing up on the link as a whole. It is good practice for a part (ii) to make reference to the contribution of scholars not mentioned in part (i).

## Kantian deontology

| | 2010 | 2011 | 2012 | 2013 |
|---|---|---|---|---|
| **Strengths and/or weaknesses** | | | | *i* |
| **No questions** | | | *x* | |
| **Important features** | *i* | *i* | | |
| **Effective as guideline for moral living** | | *ii* | | |
| **Persuasive or not** | *ii* | | | *ii (a)* |

*(a) "in modern world"*

▸ **Part (i) Analysis**

**Important features**

According to the examiner's reports, the best answers will be structured around the key features of Kant's philosophy, which may include duty, absolutism, goodwill and rationality, as opposed to morality being based on consequences or emotional responses. Likewise, they will highlight the prominence of the categorical imperative (and its three forms, illustrated concisely by use of examples), and contrast it with a hypothetical imperative, rather than simply rattling off descriptions of each type. A more advanced answer will explain why Kant saw moral statements as being "a priori-synthetic" and that he saw the supreme goal for humans as the achievement of the "summum bonum"; his three postulates of pure practical reason - autonomy, immortality of the soul, his four principles of right action and the necessary existence of God.

Pitfalls to avoid:

- Common errors including stating that Kant did not believe in God and/or that he supported both hypothetical and categorical imperatives.

- Listing postulates, principles and definitions; let the question shape your use of material.

- Referring to "reason" as meaning having "a reason to act" rather than morality being based on rational thought.

- Giving only one form of the categorical imperative - some are less well known among students, particularly the "Formula of the Kingdom of Ends".

- Selecting examples or anecdotes because they are easy to remember, rather than for their relevance, for example, the scenario of the shopkeeper and people with red hair.

### Strengths and/or weaknesses

The 2013 question asks for the strengths in part (i), so try to structure your response around these. For example, you can use the strength of it being deontological to discuss its a priori nature.

### ▸ Part (ii) Analysis

### Effective as guideline for moral living (2011)

You need to give strong arguments (supported by reason or evidence) both for and against the effectiveness of the theory as a guideline for moral living. Arguments for, mentioned in the examiner's report, include the fact that Kant's maxim of universality protects human rights and his deontological approach is similar to that of Natural Law, so it could be supported by some religious believers. You could utilise biblical material that emphasises duty, such as the Ten Commandments (Exodus 20), and the Good Samaritan. You could develop your response by reference to Ross, and show how his prima facie approach helps to overcome the issue of conflicting duties.

Pitfalls to avoid:

- Giving very simplistic reasons as to why Kant's thought might or might not be an effective guideline for morality, for example that Kant's approach is cold or heartless in its neglect of emotions or consequences.

- Or that his deontological approach was good as it provided rules to follow: A better approach might compare or contrast Kant's with the other religious and ethical outlooks studied at AS level.

### Persuasive or not (2010, 2013)

There are two interesting tenets of this question; the first being the use of the word "persuasive". You could explore for whom the theory may be persuasive, for example, realists/anti-realists; religious believers/agnostics/atheists, and in reference to particular issues, environments or institutions, like medical ethics or schools.

The second tenet is the phrase "in the modern world". It would be interesting to consider whether the zeitgeist of modern philosophy might find Kantian deontology hard or easy to accept; and also whether in your opinion, there may be modern dilemmas which would or would not benefit from Kantian principles.

## Natural Moral Law

|  | 2010 | 2011 | 2012 | 2013 |
|---|---|---|---|---|
| **Strengths and/or weaknesses** |  |  |  | *i* |
| **Key features (ideas)** | *i* | *i* | *i* |  |
| **Undermined by critiques of R&M** |  | *ii* |  |  |
| **Persuasive or not** | *ii* |  | *ii* | *ii (a)* |

*(a) "in modern world"*

### ▸ Part (i) Analysis

**Key features/ideas (2010, 2011, 2012)**

*A good answer might begin by placing the theory in its philosophical context; for example, recognising that Natural Moral Law is a deontological theory, with a teleological aspect. The response should then swiftly proceed with a focus on the key features, which may include actions being intrinsically right or wrong; use of reason to identify primary and secondary precepts, interior and exterior acts, real and apparent goods, cardinal and theological virtues. - Examiner's Report*

You should draw on the thinking of prominent scholars, whilst maintaining a focus on key features, for example, the idea of purpose in the writings of Aristotle, and the four types of interrelated law outlined by Aquinas, trying to show development from one to the other. It is also good practice to pick up on key features regarding the underpinning of the arguments, for example, recognising that Aquinas saw rational thought as a God-given ability, and fulfilling that purpose is "good".

Pitfalls to avoid:

- Only learning one ethical theory, for example only learning on deontology in June 2012.

- Simply listing the strengths and weaknesses of Natural Moral Law.

- Spending time giving irrelevant background information on Aristotle or Aquinas.

- Ignoring the secondary precepts, or referring to them inaccurately, for example as being absolutist, which they are not.

- Confusing "real" and "apparent" goods with "interior" and "exterior" acts.

### Strengths and/or weaknesses (2013)

The 2013 question asks for the strengths in part (i), so try to structure your response around these. For example, you can use the strength of it being deontological with a teleological aspect to discuss its primary and secondary precepts, making links with scholars and examples. You may also consider the perception that it is tangible in its appeal to nature, which is an aspect of the theory that can be easily developed.

**Persuasive or not (2010, 2012, 2013)**

The key to unlocking this question is surely to consider what would make a theory persuasive, for example, how practical it is; how applicable it is to modern scenarios, whether it tends to lead to pleasing outcomes or not. Another question to address is who the theory might be persuasive for: theists; atheists; agnostics; as well as traditionalists and others with preconceived thought-frames, such as realists and anti-realists. You should evaluate what is and isn't persuasive about the chosen theory, through reference to scholars and tightly expressed examples. You could also draw on material from AS as a contrasting approach. The 2013 question uses the phrase "in the modern world", so do not ignore this aspect.

Pitfalls to avoid:

- Structuring your answers in terms of a list of strengths then a list of weaknesses, followed by a brief conclusion.

- Giving an opinion based rather than argument-based conclusion, for example, expressing scorn of the theory because of its opposition to homosexuality and its masculine bias, instead of grappling with the question and producing a mature and thought-provoking response.

**Undermined by critiques of religion and morality (2011)**

A good answer will recognise the relevance of this link, by stressing the links between religion and NML in a specific way that highlights key issues, before evaluating specifically whether each one has or has not been successfully undermined by critiques.

Pitfall to avoid:

- Ignoring the question set, and instead offering a prepared answer on the critiques of the link between religion and morality, based largely around the ideas of Richard Dawkins.

## Virtue Ethics

|  | 2010 | 2011 | 2012 | 2013 |
|---|---|---|---|---|
| **Key ideas (features)** |  | *i* | *i* | *i (a)* |
| **Effective as guideline for moral living** |  | *ii* |  |  |
| **Successful or not** |  |  | *ii* |  |
| **No questions** | *x* |  |  |  |

*(a) ii R&M*

▸ **Part (i) Analysis**

**Key ideas (features)**

A solid approach will provide a brief background to Virtue Ethics, for example, recognising that it is concerned with exploring the question "What sort of person should I become?", and acknowledging its basis in Aristotle's quest to find the virtues that make good people good, and cultivating identified virtues so that humans can achieve their ultimate aim of eudaimonia. You could then develop various other key features of the theory, recognising how it has been developed by scholars who have rejected the modern approach to ethics, believing that a return to person-centred ethics would be beneficial for all. You can refer to MacIntyre's ideas of "goods internal" and "external goods" as well as his ideas regarding the three types of character that emerged in this current "moral vacuum". You should also focus on Anscombe as well as other modern scholars such as Franklin, Foot and Nussbaum, and not base your whole answer on Aristotle. An A-grader will not only be able to analyse a number of key features and ideas, but find links between them, so that their answer reads as a whole.

You would also do well to show knowledge and understanding of:

- Aristotle's concept of the soul and how the concept of the soul was linked to the different types of virtues.

- The moral and intellectual virtues, including the doctrine of the mean and how these virtues were fostered through habit or instruction.

- The importance of "perfect" friendships in helping to foster these virtues and how the development of the virtues could lead to the development of better communities.

Pitfalls to avoid:

- Including irrelevant material such as a detailed historical background of Aristotle or information about Greek philosophy in general.

- Writing everything you know about virtue ethics.

- Failing to link ideas, such as the doctrine of the mean, the soul, and types of friendship into a coherent theory.

- Misunderstanding certain aspects, for example stating that the doctrine of the mean applies to both the intellectual and moral virtues which is not the case - it applies to the moral virtues only.

### ▸ Part (ii) Analysis

#### Effective as guideline for moral living

You need to consider whether the starting point, the virtues, is indeed a good guide for moral living. Reasons and evidence to support this claim might include the fact that Virtue Theory allows humankind to flourish. Reasons against might include Kant's view that the development of the virtues cannot be the supreme goal of morality because even an evil person could sometimes act in a courageous manner.

Pitfalls to avoid:

- Failing to address the question.

- Writing simplistic answers, arguing that Virtue Ethics helps make you a good person or that it doesn't give you clear guidelines to follow.

#### Successful or not

As with many part (ii) questions, you will do well to consider how a theory might be successful, and who the theory may be successful for. You may consider, for example, that some religious adherents might reject Aristotle's approach as it is not deontological, then go on to expound that it failed to recognise the concept of Divine Authority and that it appeared to be concerned with self-fulfilment rather than the altruistic approach taken by most religions. (Examiner's Report, 2012) You may refer to other theories from other areas of the course, to compare success in a particular area.

Pitfall to avoid:

- Structuring your answer as a list of strengths then a list of weaknesses, followed by a brief open-based conclusion writing a one-sided response.

## Justice, law and punishment

|  | 2010 | 2011 | 2012 | 2013 |
|---|---|---|---|---|
| **Key ideas (important concepts)** | *i* | *i (one)* | *i* | *i* |
| **Objectivity and/or subjectivity** | *ii* | *ii* | *ii* | *ii* |

Want to stand out from the crowd? Consider this challenge:

*Despite a few strong responses to this question, it continues to be the least popular and to attract some of the weakest responses. - Examiner's Report, 2011*

▸ **Part (i) Analysis**

**Key ideas (important concepts)**

You need to be very clear on whether the question asks for a discussion of all three (2010, 2012, 2013), or one of the three (2011).

**ALL THREE (2010, 2012, 2013)** - The best answers will be able to relate the central ideas of these topics to a range of scholars and concepts, whilst maintaining a tight, coherent style. You may wish to utilise arguments from Rawls, Locke, Plato, Hobbes, Moore, Dawkins, Newman and Bentham, or you could take a theme-based approach, engaging with various versions of the Social Contract in relation to the three areas. The key is to show links between the these areas, and there are good ways and excellent ways to do this.

*The majority of responses dealt with the ideas on law and punishment and how law can be seen as objective, whilst punishment is generally subjective. Stronger responses discussed these ideas using examples drawn from other disciplines, eg sociology or history, and debating the changing nature of law and punishment across societies and generations. - Examiner's Report, 2010*

A good answer may explore the issue of capital punishment in the UK and USA, but stronger answers will also consider corporal punishment.

Pitfalls to avoid:

- Ignoring one of the three, particularly law or justice.

- Focusing only on elementary ideas in justice or punishment.

- Failing to make any link between these three concepts, leading to a disjointed piece.

- Listing views of scholars about justice, without making use of that information to construct an argument.

- Becoming obsessed with the financial differential between capital punishment and life imprisonment. (Examiner's Report, 2010)

**ONE OF THE THREE (2011)** - You obviously need to make your choice clear; stick to it, and examine it in depth of scholarship. For example, you could make good use of Nozick's idea of Justice as Entitlement vs Rawl's idea of Justice as Fairness. Inclusion of Plato, Hobbes, Locke and Mill could all feature well.

Pitfalls to avoid:

- Combining justice and punishment rather than following the instructions in the question to make a choice.

- Writing an answer lacking in scholarly detail; law and punishment received its fair share of GCSE-level descriptions about capital punishment and various methods of punishments meted out by society. (Examiner's Report, 2011)

▸ **Part (ii) Analysis**

**Objectivity and/or subjectivity**

A question of this type should come as no surprise! In your preparation on these three topics, you should have a firm grasp of these concepts, and where each response stands in relation to them.

Pitfalls to avoid:

- Explaining the concepts in a generic way, for example, "relativism was mostly associated with cross-cultural issues to express divergent views" (2012); "confusing subjectivism and objectivism and mainly talking about relativism" (2010).

- Giving one-sided answers.

## Ethical language

|  | 2010 | 2011 | 2012 | 2013 |
|---|---|---|---|---|
| **Problems with use and/or meaning** |  | *i* | *i* | *i* |
| **Contribution of emotivism** | *i* |  |  |  |
| **Problems solved or unsolved** | *ii* | *ii* |  |  |
| **Success or otherwise** |  |  | *ii* | *ii* |

▸ **Part (i) Analysis**

**Problems with use and/or meaning (2011, 2012, 2013)**

It would not be hard to get a little confused about which material you should put in part (i) and part (ii) respectively. One report suggest the following:

*... that you focus on the problems of language in part (i), and save theories as solutions to the problems in part (ii).*

Problems: the definition of "good"; the concept of the "is-ought" gap; the naturalistic fallacy.

However, the temptation with following this structure is to write more for part (ii) than part (i), and that would be very unwise. Hence you will need to include some material on ethical language here. This may include some key words, features and theories within this area, which do not tread on the toes of your part (ii) material.

Pitfalls to avoid:

- Confusing the terms "analytic" and "synthetic".

- Discussing the naturalistic fallacy without fully understanding it "within its context and milieu". (Examiner's Report, 2011)

- Confusing religious and ethical language.

## Contribution of emotivism

A question such as this is a stark reminder that you need to have mastered knowledge of adequate detail on the main theories, especially emotivism. You should explore issues around emotivism, main contributors and features, but expand your study through placing it within the context of the debate as a whole. You might consider the value of Logical Positivism and key scholars from the Vienna Circle, such as Moore, Singer, Vardy and even Tyler.

Pitfalls to avoid:

- Dealing only briefly with emotivism.

- Not been able to distinguish between religious language (eg God) and ethical language (eg good).

*Make sure you are prepared to write specifically about emotivism in an essay on ethical language as it is named in the specification as a particular focus of this topic. - Examiner's Report, 2010*

**Problems solved or unsolved (2011, 2012, 2013)/Success or otherwise (2010)**

A successful approach might be to reserve intuitionism, emotivism and/or Ayer's verification principle for use here, instead of using it in part (i).

You may wish to:

- engage with the concept of "good"

- explore the development of emotivism through the work of Hume and the Logical Positivists

- discuss the verification principle together with the terms "analytic", "synthetic" and "meaningless" statements

- recognise that Ayer saw ethical statements as non-factual - simply an expression of emotion - and that his work was later developed by Stevenson and again by Hare's prescriptivism

- address intuitionism confidently

- engage with Pritchard's prescriptivism.

However, the presentation of this material must be evaluative, hence you need to discuss the success or otherwise of each idea as a solution to the problems of ethical language. One thought to consider is how to successfully end your part (ii). Of ending on a succinct and relevant quotation, one examiner's report says: "This is a very useful device which lends a real air of authority to your writing."

Pitfalls to avoid:

- Repeating material from part (i) without adding much evaluative comment.

- Rewriting the question to focus on intuitionism, to the detriment of other approaches.

- Only referring to emotivism in general terms, and calling it the "boo/hurrah" theory without explaining why it is often called this, implying in some cases that this was Ayer's own term for it.

# UNIT 4 IMPLICATIONS (EDEXCEL 6RS04)

## QUESTION 1B - PHILOSOPHY OF RELIGION

The past questions include sections from the following readings:

|          | 2010 | 2011 | 2012 | 2013 |
|----------|------|------|------|------|
| **Ayer**     |      |      |      | ✓    |
| **Westphal** |      | ✓    |      |      |
| **Donovan**  | ✓    |      | ✓    |      |

## *June 2010*

*"Why all this talk about arguing from religious experience?." "If you really experience God you don't have to argue, you know he's real, and that's all there is to it." So if we are trying to do justice to the varieties of religious experience, we must take seriously this particular type, the sense of knowledge arising from inner conviction. It is a risky business, of course, to claim to know something and to act as though one knows for sure, if one can't give much in the way of reasons for one's claim ... To have no doubts at all about one's beliefs may sometimes be more a symptom of insanity or arrogant irresponsibility than of sound thinking. Yet believers, aware of all of these risks, may still feel they have a right to say they know because they experience God's reality for themselves. - Source: P Donovan (2000) Can we know God by experience? In B Davies (ed) Philosophy of Religion: a guide and anthology, Oxford University Press, p113*

## ▸ 1 (a) Examine the argument and/or interpretation in the passage (30)

You should be able to summarise the argument put forward in the passage, namely the claim that a serious argument for the existence of God is based on the sense of knowing God, arising from inner conviction. You should "contextualise" your answer by setting out when and how it has gained momentum, and with whom it is popular or controversial. You could also look at the philosophical context, namely, its basis in a posteriori thinking, as well as its discussion of the concepts of intuition and knowledge. Your answer may deal swiftly and effectively with key contributors to this argument, and an assessment of the strength or otherwise of different types of religious experience. Other scholars should be drawn upon to highlight the risks and problems associated with this argument. These can be drawn from the rest of the article, as well as your wider reading in Units 1-3 and the rest of the anthology.

Pitfalls to avoid:

- Writing a descriptive and basic account of the passage akin to a simple comprehension test.

- Ignoring the extract altogether, and generalising about the Donovan article as a whole (see above section How to Analyse the Specification: Unit 4).

- Spending too long on Unit 3-style material on religious experience at the expense of a more detailed analysis of the passage itself or on the distinct views of Donovan.

▸ **(b) Do you agree with the idea(s) expressed? Justify your point of view and discuss its implications for understanding religion and human experience. (20)**

You need to come to your own conclusion either before or after your analysis of the views of scholars who both support and oppose the argument put forward in the passage. Notable scholars mentioned in the mark scheme are Hick, Goulder, Swinburne and Sharpe, but also praised was the approach that sets out a personal view, allying it or contrasting it with scholars drawn upon from Units 1-3 or the rest of the Unit 4 anthology.

*The better quality answers were those that expressed viewpoints with confidence and authority, supported by reason and evidence. - Examiner's Report*

You can debate Donovan's ideas about "knowledge" and notions about "having no doubts", as well as explore the links and contrasts with the a priori reasoning found in the ontological argument. It would also be advantageous to recognise that some of Donovan's points relate to religious language claims and for this you can make use of the views of AJ Ayer and verification together with a range of relevant ideas in Westphal's article. The examiner's report also praises an approach that made links with intuitionism and GE Moore.

In terms of the implications for religion, you can consider the impact of your conclusions on use of religious language, as well as the status of religious experience and intuition as adequate basis for belief. You may like to ask yourself the following questions:

- How does an exploration of the differences between feeling certain and being right affect how I approach philosophical discussion about matters of faith?

- Should religious belief be based merely on experience, not at all or partially?

- What religious practices, scriptures and statements are philosophically sound or unjustifiable, according to my conclusions?

The views of Wittgenstein, and the anti-realists, may be expounded here, and it may be helpful to conclude whether an anti-realist approach to matters of religion is all that is left (Donovan doesn't think so), and if it is, does that weaken or strengthen religious belief? What are the implications for the atheist, theist or agnostic?

In terms of human experience, you could consider the a posteriori nature of the argument, and ask how your conclusions about basing belief on experience or intuition affects your acceptance or otherwise of other types of knowledge, for example in the area of ethics. Can you link anti-realism with moral relativity? The mark scheme also suggests you could compare the epistemological view that knowledge can be based on inner conviction with reference to a correspondence theory. The examiner's report ends this section by praising an approach that places this passage in a broader perspective so as to debate implications from history, politics and contemporary issues.

Pitfalls to avoid:

- Writing about other scholars and material without rooting ideas in the extract or views of Donovan; you must make your links explicit and relevant.

- Taking the view quoted above ("If you really experience God you don't have to argue, you know he's real, and that's all there is to it"), and assuming it to be the view of Donovan. You need to show an awareness of where his view comes out in his conclusion. An example of good practice given in the examiner report summarises the eventual conclusion of Donovan, in the opening paragraph.

- Not spending adequate time teasing out the implications for religion AND human experience.

## June 2011

*Modern Philosophy of Religion grew out of a deep dissatisfaction with historic Christianity. But the response of Hume and his followers was very different from that of Kant and his followers. Instead of seeking an alternative religion, inoffensive to modernity, they looked to see whether the problem might not lie at the very heart of religion and not in the disposable husks. Suspicion, rather than scepticism, arises when instead of asking about the evidence for or against religious beliefs one asks what motives underlie religious beliefs and practices, and what functions they play in the lives of believers. In The Natural History of Religion Hume develops a notion of instrumental religion according to which piety is primarily a flattering of the gods grounded in selfish hopes and fears. The piety of self-interest immediately gives rise to self-deception, since the pious soul cannot acknowledge that it has reduced the sacred to nothing but a means to its own ends. - Source: M Westphal (2002) The Emergence of Modern Philosophy of Religion in P Quinn and C Taliaferro (eds) - A Companion to Philosophy of Religion, Blackwell, p132*

## ▸ 1 (a) Examine the argument and/or interpretation in the passage (30)

A good start commended by the examiners is to present a brief overview of the whole source before quickly focusing on the selected passage. You need to show you have a clear grasp of the background to the debate, particularly the context of the Enlightenment. You should show a depth and/or breadth of understanding about the key issues, namely; the transition from philosophical theology to philosophy of religion; the contrast between suspicion and scepticism; clarification of key terms such a "kernel" and "husk"; a clear and critical analysis of Kantian ideas of pure practical reason, Hume's distinction between evidence and motives and instrumental religion, as well as his reference to selected aspects of the Natural History of Religion. When discussing these ideas it is important to show a clear distinction between the views of Hume and Kant.

Additionally you may move into different elements in your studies, such as other critiques of religion found in Units 1-3, for example Freud and Marx, the other readings in the anthology, and the rest of Westphal's article (provided you ground it in this extract). Examiners praised approaches that mainly focused on Kant and Hume, but also those that some presented informed analysis of a range of scholars such as Aquinas, Durkheim, Hegel, Nietzsche and Schleiermacher. Use of contributions from Dawkins and Kierkegaard was received well, but they must be used intelligently.

Pitfalls to avoid:

- Preparing "a generic response to Westphal that provided only incidental information on the extract itself. For example by having insufficient focus on the ideas associated with suspicion of religion in comparison to scepticism". (Examiner's Report)

- Writing more on other scholars (such as Ayer and Donovan), rather than Westphal himself.

- Not referring to other scholars and debates in reference to the ideas within the passage.

- Spending too long on Unit 3-type arguments for the existence of God, rather than the specific debates and issues within the extract.

*All of these topics are worthwhile to explore, but not when it becomes a substitute for answering the specific passage. - Examiner's Report*

## ▸ (b) Do you agree with the idea(s) expressed? Justify your point of view and discuss its implications for understanding religion and human experience. (20)

Using scholarly debates and comparisons of strengths and weaknesses, you should critique agreement with Hume and Kant on the problem with, or origins of, religion. Some helpful questions to ask yourself here may be: Do you agree with Hume's perception of instrumental religion? Should suspicion, rather than scepticism, be allowed to guide questions of religion? You may choose another point of view altogether, such as one that upholds or seeks to justify the heart of religion, or one that not only rejects the heart, but the husks as well. It is important that your arguments here are grounded in academic debate, and that your writing is clear, coherent and well-structured.

*Implications were worked out in relation to specific groups such as theist, atheist and agnostic with reference to specific scholars such as Ayer and Wittgenstein. - Examiner's Report*

You may like to consider the implications for religion if its problems lie at its very heart; does this change it unrecognisably? Does this render it useless? Is there more to religious belief than fear and self-interest? If so, what? Kant's moral argument for the existence of God may be helpful to refer to here, as well as reference to Life after Death (Unit 3). You may like to consider whether religion based purely on feelings of fear and selfishness render it meaningless, or whether it may still fulfil a function.

For implications related to human experience, it may be appropriate to consider whether knowledge based on suspicion rather than scepticism affects other areas of thought and practice, for example, Ethics and Philosophy.

Pitfalls to avoid:

- Not being specific enough about your own point of view.

- Giving random thoughts, rather than scholarly implications.

- Using the topic to have a rant about your own brand of theism, atheism or agnosticism; all arguments must be rigorously academic.

## June 2012

*The chief point of the philosophical criticisms of 'knowing God by experience' amounts to this. Where popular religious reasoning falls down is not in taking the sense of God too seriously, but in trying to treat it as a form of knowledge, of a self-certifying kind, immediately available to those who have it. Knowledge, the philosophers point out, is just not like that - whether it is knowledge of God or of anything else. The sense of knowing is never on its own a sufficient sign of knowledge. (That distinction is a key to many of the philosophical difficulties in claims to know God by experience.) But if the sense of God fails, in the end, to count as knowledge of God, what is to be said about it? Is it of no further philosophical interest and to be discarded, like a pricked balloon, as being simply a great illusion? Nothing that has been said here leads to that conclusion. There is no justification for taking such an all-or-nothing view of religious experience (even though at times both philosophical critics and religious thinkers are inclined to do so). - Source: P Donovan (2002) Can we know God by experience? In B Davies (ed) Philosophy of Religion: a guide and anthology, Oxford University Press*

## ▸ 1 (a) Examine the argument and/or interpretation in the passage. (30)

The mark scheme stresses the need to focus on specific issues raised in the passage, whilst showing an awareness of the whole Donovan reading, background issues and a detailed grasp of the key ideas and terms that feature in the debate. "This may include reference to some principles underlying related arguments such as the principle of credulity (mark scheme), as well as material from other units, such as the design and cosmological arguments (Unit 1), the argument from religious experience (Unit 3) and the other Unit 4 texts."

A paper that was highlighted as an example of good practice had a short and strong introduction that used compelling phrases like "the essential point is ..." This gives the examiner confidence you are on the right track!

You should draw on key scholars referred to by Donovan in the wider passage, such as Owen and Buber, as well as other relevant philosophers, such as Swinburne, Tillich and Ward. Be sure to show an awareness of the thrust of the issue, notably, his diagnosis of the mistake made by those who say they "just know God exists"; that of treating self-certifying experiential knowledge of God as a form of knowledge like any other. From this, you can then tease out the impact Donovan's conclusion has on the argument from religious experience.

Top Tip: The examiners were impressed by students who were "able to use the extract as a springboard to showcase their wider philosophical knowledge ... for example ... (linking the passage with) ideas about religious language and also existentialism". (Examiner's Report)

Pitfalls to avoid:

- Being too general, for example, writing about religious experience as a whole, or even focusing on the views of Ayer, rather than Donovan's main points.

- Scholar name-dropping with little detail about their contribution to the debate in hand.

- Not enough time given over to part (a).

- Set, regurgitated answers that fail to structure responses according to the section given.

**(b) Do you agree with the idea(s) expressed? Justify your point of view and discuss its implications for understanding religion and human experience. (20)**

I found both the mark scheme and examiner's report rather general here, and so I will begin with some of my own reflections. It is important to recognise that unusually, Donovan has come to a rather balanced conclusion - this is obvious in his phrase "there is no justification for taking such an all-or-nothing view of religious experience". Therefore, it is extremely important that you assess and evaluate the extreme points of view he has rejected, notably, that knowledge of God can be treated as a form of knowledge like other forms of knowledge you can "just know". Or alternatively, that rejection of considering God-knowledge in this way renders religious experience a completely useless philosophical study. The examiner report suggests that reference to Wittgenstein, Ayer, Hare and Dawkins will be smiled upon here.

In terms of evaluating the implications for religion, you may like to consider what does and doesn't constitute good grounds for religious belief. In my opinion, an interesting reflection would be a comparison of the longevity, depth and quality of faith based purely, partially or not at all on religious experience.

From the perspective of human experience, you may like to consider that the phenomena of religious experience requires cautious interpretation, or should be treated as merely subjective. There are links here with psychology and sociology - people who hear voices telling them to do harm on one extreme, or hard rationalists who reject all forms of experience as another.

Pitfalls to avoid:

- Not saving enough time for in-depth exploration of the implications for religion and human experience.

- Using part (b) to "sell your own brand of atheism, agnosticism or theism" - your answer must be more academic and focused than that!

- Waffling without relation to scholarly debates and key philosophical terminology.

- Rushing answers, so bullet-pointing or jotting points down without paragraph linking and a good solid finish.

## June 2013

*It is now generally admitted, at any rate by philosophers, that the existence of a being having the attributes which define the god of any non-animistic religion cannot be demonstratively proved. What is not so generally recognised is that there can be no way of proving that the existence of a god, such as the God of Christianity, is even probable. Yet this is also easily shown. For if the existence of such a god were probable, then the proposition that he existed would be an empirical hypothesis. And in that case it would be possible to deduce from it, and other empirical hypotheses, certain experiential propositions which were not deducible from those other hypotheses alone. But in fact this is not possible. It is sometimes claimed, indeed, that the existence of a certain sort of regularity in nature constitutes sufficient evidence for the existence of a god. But if the sentence "God exists" entails no more than that certain types of phenomena occur in certain sequences, then to assert the existence of a god will be simply equivalent to asserting that there is the requisite regularity in nature; and no religious man would admit that this was all he intended to assert in asserting the existence of a god. - Source: AJ Ayer - God-talk is evidently nonsense. In B Davies (ed)  (2000) Philosophy of Religion: a guide and anthology, Oxford University Press p119, Edexcel anthology*

▸ **1 (a) Examine the argument and/or interpretation in the passage. (30)**

According to the mark scheme, strong answers will clearly set out the background to the debate - ie the Logical Positivism of AJ Ayer, along with its empirical foundation (consider the influence of Hume), as well as informed analysis of analytic and synthetic propositions. You should also be tuned in to the influence of the "early" Wittgenstein on Ayer's thinking, in particular, the "picture theory of meaning".

Key ideas and scholarly arguments mentioned in the passage should then be discussed in detail, in particular, the difference between proof and probability and the view in the passage "that experiential propositions were not deducible from those other hypotheses alone". You may also explore relevant features of **THE ARGUMENT FROM DESIGN**, notably, the verification principle. Or given Ayer's reference to the view that the existence of God cannot be "demonstratively proved", it may be appropriate to explore the a priori features of **THE ONTOLOGICAL ARGUMENT**. Additionally, you should try to weave in views from the other two readings, (especially Westphal) and highlight how they relate to Ayer's views.

Pitfalls to avoid:

- Too much Unit 3-type religious experience material.

- Don't assume that the whole of Ayer's Language, Truth and Logic was focused on religious language. This part is found towards the end of his sixth chapter, following his critique of ethics.

> ### (b) Do you agree with the idea(s) expressed? Justify your point of view and discuss its implications for understanding religion and human experience. (20)

Your aim with part (b) is to justify your point of view through evaluating the arguments for and against the view given in the passage, weighing up strengths and weaknesses of the arguments. You may wish to begin by stating your point of view, followed by giving reasons for it, as well as the reasons you have rejected the alternative view(s) you have discussed in your answer to part (a). Philips, Dawkins, Flew, James, Swinburne and Wittgenstein are all cited as helpful scholars in assessing the acceptability of views.

It may be helpful to choose a view from the following: a rejection of Ayer's views, an acceptance of Ayer's views, or a halfway house that argues for a basic acceptance of his claims, with the development of other scholars such as Flew. The latter approach is praised by examiners as "an interesting subtle approach". In support of Ayer's view, you may want to include Hume's critique of the design hypothesis. In contrast to Ayer's view, you could include criticisms of the limitations of his account of language, and the views of the later Wittgenstein (see his work Philosophical Investigations, where he views his early work as "dogmatic"; functional theory).

In discussing the implications for religion, those who disagree with Ayer may like to consider that religious belief is more than language claims, as seen in the work of Eliade and sacred times and sacred places. Or you could take Freud's approach that religion should be viewed as illusory.

According to the examiner's report, there were interesting debates about the implications from Ayer's analysis of religious language to the way agnostics and atheists use God-talk. They also said: "A few drew attention to ignosticism which could be a fruitful way of highlighting some distinctive features of Ayer."

In terms of implications for human experience the mark scheme suggests that some types of religious experience may be beneficial such as James and the "sick soul". You may also debate the view that according to Dawkins religious belief is like a virus to be eliminated. You could concentrate on sociological implications or philosophical ones, or locate Ayer's contributions in Westphal's scheme on the shift from philosophical theology to the philosophy of religion.

Pitfalls to avoid:

- Lacking focus on the passage itself.

- Repeating or not moving beyond A01 material.

- Not giving an explicit point of view.

- Ignoring or spending insufficient time on implications.

# QUESTION 1C - ETHICS

The past questions include sections from the following readings:

|  | 2010 | 2011 | 2012 | 2013 |
|---|---|---|---|---|
| **LaFollette** | ✓ | | | |
| **Schneewind** | | ✓ | | ✓ |
| **Jamieson** | | | ✓ | |

## June 2010

*We can develop neither the moral knowledge nor empathy crucial for an impartial morality unless we have been in intimate relationships. Someone reared by uncaring parents, who never established close personal ties with others, will simply not know how to look after or promote the interests of either intimates or strangers. No one knows how to do mathematics or to play football without acquaintance with the discipline or the game. Likewise, no one knows how to consider the interests of others unless they have been in an intimate relationship ... Though I expect we may have some biologically inherited sympathetic tendencies, these will not be developed adequately unless others have cared for us and we have cared for them. If we are not motivated to promote the needs of our families or friends, how can we be motivated to promote the needs of a stranger? On the other hand, if we develop empathy toward our friends, we will be inclined to generalise it to others. We become so vividly aware of our intimate's needs that we are willing to help them even when it is difficult to do so. But since empathy is often non-specific, we will be likewise inclined to "feel" pain in acquaintances and strangers. Having felt it, we are more likely to do something about it. - Source: H LaFollette (2004) Personal Relationships in P Singer (ed) A Companion to Ethics, Blackwell p144*

▶ **(a) Examine the argument and/or interpretation in the passage. (30)**

The examiners say that you must demonstrate a "thorough grasp of the extract, either within the context of the wider passage from which it is drawn or as a stand-alone passage". However, as this passage comes as a conclusion to a wider debate I think it would be neglectful not to show an awareness of the alternative views discussed thus far; that is, that people should remain impartial in moral decision making, or show partiality to their nearest and dearest. From analysis of these two views and their shortcomings, LaFollette comes to the conclusion that impartial morality is dependent on having learned about morality from within the context of intimate relationships, and it is this central idea within the passage which warrants the bulk of your discussion. Helpful topics to explore within this area may include; the idea that morality is based on rules which need to be learned rather than instinct; the idea of emotional empathy leading to appropriate moral responses. Are these assumptions justified?

In addition to an in-depth exploration of the LaFollette passage, you should also make links with the other readings in the anthology, especially Jamieson. I also think you could make some interesting links between the passage and the other units, particularly religion and morality, and the ethical theories.

Pitfalls to avoid:

- As always, giving a descriptive and basic account of the passage rather than analysis and argument.

- Ignoring the key terms within the passage. Phrases such as "moral knowledge", "empathy" and "impartial morality" need unpacking in order to show "crystal clear" understanding.

▸ **(b) Do you agree with the idea(s) expressed? Justify your point of view and discuss its implications for understanding religion and human experience. (20)**

This passage proffers some interesting answers to some big ethical questions, such as those about the nature of morality, how it develops, and the nature of the conflict between partial and impartial morality. You could pick one of these questions to answer, or incorporate a response to all three as you clearly express whether you agree with LaFollette's position. Don't forget to give reasons why you have rejected alternatives, drawing on various theories and the views of scholars as you go. Peter Singer may be useful here, as he argues for an impartial utilitarianism. In contrast, the commandment to "Honour your father and Mother" (Exodus 20:12), which features in Divine Command Theory, gives familial relationships a special significance. (Although see also Leviticus 23:22.)

*The better quality answers were those that expressed viewpoints with confidence and authority supported by reason and evidence. - Examiner's Report*

For religious implications, it may be interesting to consider the impact of your conclusions on key biblical and Church doctrines, such as original sin, the role of conscience and duty to family and friends as well as neighbours and the stranger.

For implications for human experience, the examiners praised academically rigorous work which made use of pertinent examples, the rest of the anthology and the other units. It would be good to consider the implications for a range of ethical theories including Utilitarianism and Situation Ethics (Unit 1), and Deontology, Natural Moral Law, Virtue Ethics and Emotivism (Unit 3). "Links were made with a commendable range of scholars such as Aquinas, Aristotle, Kant, MacIntyre and Ross." (Examiner's Report)  However, you need to remain rooted in the passage with one foot, whilst stepping into a broader perspective with the other. This might mean including implications from history, politics, and other pertinent issues, such as a comparison between the ideas of Freud and Popper contrasted in an essay showcased in the examiner's report as an example of good practice.

Pitfalls to avoid:

- As always, not working through the demands of part b in turn: a point of view with justification; implications for religion; implications for human experience.

- Presenting basic accounts of ethical theories such as Utilitarianism and Situation Ethics without choosing the relevant and concise aspects which made clear links with the extract.

- Vague phrases such as: "I believe that most people have such strong feelings ..." Your views should be supported by evidence and reason with reference to scholarship.

## June 2011

*Ancient Western philosophical thought about how to live centred on the question of the highest good: what life is most fully and lastingly satisfying? While virtue was meant to govern one's relations with others, it was first of all the condition of attaining the good for oneself. Christianity taught that the highest good was attainable only through salvation, and complicated the pursuit of it by insisting on obedience to God's commands. The distinctive enterprise of modern philosophical ethics grew as ideas of the highest good and of the will of the Christian deity came to seem less and less able to provide practical guidance. Since many people today do not believe, as the ancients did, that there is just one definite way of living which is best for everyone, and since many think we cannot resolve our practical problems on a religious basis, the questions of modern Western ethics are unavoidably still our own questions. - Source: J Schneewind (2001) Modern Moral Philosophy in P Singer (ed) A Companion to Ethics, Blackwell, p147*

▸ **(a) Examine the argument and/or interpretation in the passage. (30)**

A good answer will focus on the key terminology in the passage as well as the key themes. Key terms include; virtue, salvation and practical guidance. Key themes may include the "highest good"; the relationship between religion and morality; and the claim that ancient forms of moral philosophy are not sufficiently diverse to be appealing to the modern ethicist. You may expand by exploring the claim that religious morality provided a definitive way of living morally which is no longer relevant to most ethical thinkers and/or ethical problems in the modern world, alongside the observation that modern ethics still presents significant problems which need to be resolved in a relevant way: If not religion, then what can guide decision making? In these discussions, you may wish to make reference to Aquinas, Aristotle, Bayle, Hobbes, Locke, Moore, Plato Rawls and Ross - all mentioned by the examiner's report.

*The more successful answers contextualised this extract in relation to the overall source. - Examiner's Report*

It is of fundamental importance to place this reading within the context of Schneewind's essay as found in the anthology. You may relate the issues in this passage to where he goes next, which is to offer a historical survey of the development of ethical theory by use of examples, as well as his conclusions about the "new directions" taken by ethics.

Additionally, you should link this extract with ethical theories from other units such as utilitarianism and deontology, emotivism and intuitionism. According to examiners, Virtue Ethics was used to good effect with both the Aristotelian and the more recent versions by Anscombe and McIntyre. Within the anthology, good connections were made with the Jamieson extract and to a lesser extent LaFollette.

Pitfalls to avoid:

- Paraphrasing generalised material with little reference to the passage or specific ethical theories.

- Ignoring key terms in the passage.

- Showing ignorance about the chronology, evolution and distinctiveness of ethical theories and scholarship. A really good grasp of the Schneewind article as a whole, together with dates and specifics, will greatly help you to avoid this pitfall.

▸ **(b) Do you agree with the idea(s) expressed? Justify your point of view and discuss its implications for understanding religion and human experience. (20)**

You need to first of all decide whether you agree with Schneewind's reflections on the nature of moral philosophy and its development - for example, you may like to agree or disagree with his claims that ideas of the highest good and of the will of the Christian deity fail to provide practical guidance, and hence the traditional approach of solving moral problems by reference to God, is null and void; furthermore, that there is not just one definite way of living which is best for everyone (humanitarians might disagree). You need to explain why you have rejected views other than your own, with reference to scholars, examples and key ideas. Dawkins, Dostoevsky, Nietzsche and Sartre are all well worth exploring in their rejection of religious morality, but you must use your own views to guide their input here, either by agreeing, disagreeing or partially accepting their views.

For religious implications, you may like to discuss where your conclusion leaves religion as a tool within moral decision making - Is it useless? Is it an intrinsic good? Is it an instrumental good? Is religion more or less relevant than Schneewind suggests? What are the implications for society of a rejection of religious morality? An interesting link here may come from Unit 1: sexual ethics and the 1960s Situation Ethics movement. Conversely, you may address the possibility that many people do continue to approach morality on a religious foundation and give examples to support this view.

When looking at the implications for human experience, you may consider the implications of embracing a diverse approach to moral decision making in the modern world; the role of virtue thinking in contemporary ethics; Schneewind's final observations about the concerns of modern moral philosophy in finding new approaches, and what the implications of some of these may be, for example in the area of politics, and other community-based concerns "including preservation of resources and the environment, population control, and the prevention of nuclear war". (Schneewind)

*June 2012*

*In my view moral theorising is something that real people do in everyday life. It is not just the domain of professors, expounding in their lecture halls. Moral theorising can be found on the highways and byways, practised by everyone from bartenders to politicians. In everyday life it is common for people to apply role-reversal tests, to appeal to possible outcomes of actions or policies, or to point to special responsibilities and obligations. This is the stuff of moral persuasion, reasoning and education.*

*For example we ask children how they would feel if they were treated as they have treated others. To an acquaintance we point out that it would not cost much to visit a sick parent, and that it would do the parent a world of good. We condemn a friend for not acting as a friend. When we ask why we should be moved by such considerations, or we test them in order to see whether they hang together with other beliefs and commitments that we have, we are engaging in moral theorising.*

*However, the result of this theorising hardly ever leads to the creation of a full-blown moral theory. Generally we are pushed into theorising by pragmatic considerations rather than by the disinterested search for truth. We are usually pushed out of it by conversational closure - one of us gets our way, or we agree to disagree. Moral theorising typically emerges when there is a conversational niche for it to fill.*

*- Source: "Method and moral theory"D Jamieson in P Singer (ed) - (2001) A Companion to Ethics (Blackwell) pp476-486 © A Companion to Ethics, P Singer (2001) Blackwell Publishers*

## 1 (a) Examine the argument and/or interpretation in the passage. (30)

Examiners praised confident work, rich in breadth and detail. Specific areas of mention were: the notion of "moral theorising"; candidates may consider whether this everyday moral theorising has any real value and whether "everyone from bartenders to politicians" realise that they are engaged in moral theorising (mark scheme, level 5). You may wish to make an academic exploration of the following statements in your answer: moral theorising is not only an academic domain; moral theorising is an important way in which we test our behaviour and the behaviour of others; moral theorising reflects the way in which moral theories have developed (mark scheme, level 4).

You may also wish to widen your discussion of the issues raised in the passage by linking it with other ideas in the Jamieson article. For example, knowledge of coherentism and foundationalism; ostensive, hypothetical and imaginary examples; the claim that until recently moral philosophers neglected questions about moral theory; the "appeal to possible outcomes". In examining such issues it is essential to return regularly to the passage, and write with an extensive use of examples, terminology and reference to a range of scholars such as Anscombe, MacIntyre, Williams and Ross.

Reference to the other sources in the anthology, notably LaFollette's discussion of whether morality should be partial or impartial, is given as an example of good practice. Relevant material from other units, especially ethical theories in Unit 1 and Unit 3, for example - the link between moral theorising and Virtue Ethics - will also gain you credit.

Pitfalls to avoid:

- Broad pre-prepared summaries of Jamieson that are not structured from and around the passage in the question.

- Generalised views on ethical theories that are not related to Jamieson.

- Misunderstanding about Jamieson's points regarding the difference between moral theory and moral theorising, or his discussion on the role of examples: these complex arguments need careful preparation.

▸ **(b) Do you agree with the idea(s) expressed? Justify your point of view and discuss its implications for understanding religion and human experience. (20)**

*In response to the question: Do you agree with the ideas expressed? Strong responses presented their own opinions and located these within their wider areas of study. - Examiner's Report*

You may consider, with use of examples, how far you agree that moral theorising goes on in everyday life, or you may consider whether you agree or disagree that moral theorising ultimately has little impact on the development of moral theory. A strong answer will give scholarly reasons for the selected views, as well as detailed, academic reasons for the views rejected.

For implications, you may make wide-ranging observations about the nature of moral philosophy and its development; for example, the impact of popular moral theorising in the media, how far religious morality engages in this kind of moral theorising, and/or you may wish to explore the motivations of this conversational moral theorising - for example, is it just to make us feel better about ourselves and our actions? You can explore the implications raised about the need for modern ethics to find new approaches to moral philosophy and to consider how successful these have been. You may also consider the implications for those who are not able or willing to engage in this conventional form of moral conversation.

Pitfalls to avoid:

- Describing different points of view rather than arguing for your point of view.

- Not exploring implications for religion AND human experience.

- Not linking paragraphs, or producing answers with grammatical disorganisation.

## June 2013

*Three concerns have marked recent developments in moral philosophy.*

1. *Much work is being done on actual social and political problems. Questions concerning abortion, environmental ethics, just war, medical treatment, business practices, the rights of animals, and the position of women and children occupy a considerable part of the literature and teaching considered to be moral philosophy or ethics.*

2. *There has been a return to the Aristotelian vision of morality as centrally a matter of virtue, rather than abstract principles. Alasdair MacIntyre and Bernard Williams, among others, attempt to develop*

*a communitarian view of moral personality and of the functioning of morality.*

3. *Finally, there has been a rapid growth of interest in the problems posed by the need to co-ordinate the behaviour of many individuals if effective action is to be taken. If too many people use a lake for a rural retreat, no one will get the solitude each desires; but one person's decision to stay away may do no good; how are we to decide what is to be done? Many issues, including preservation of resources and the environment, population control, and the prevention of nuclear war seem to have similar structure, and moral philosophers along with economists, mathematicians and others are being drawn to them.*

*- Source: adapted from "Modern moral philosophy" (2001) J Schneewind in P Singer (ed) A Companion to Ethics (Blackwell) pp147–156, Edexcel Anthology p153*

## ▶ 1 (a) Examine the argument and/or interpretation in the passage. (30)

This passage provides a really helpful three-fold structure to your response, and a good way to approach this question would be to deal with each one in turn, relating them to the rest of the article, as well as other readings in the anthology and the other units, especially the ethical theories in Unit 3. Make sure you explore, with proficiency, the key terms and key themes within the passage, such as virtue ethics and communitarianism (as opposed to individualism in morality). You may also like to make reference to Rawls' observation that the problems of justice cannot be resolved by decisions individuals make separately. Reference to Aristotle, Kant, MacIntyre, Mill and Williams were mentioned as praiseworthy by examiners.

Additionally, the mark scheme indicates that you may unpack further the claim that there has been a return to Aristotelian ideas of morality; why there has been a rapid growth of interest in the problems posed by the need to co-ordinate the behaviour of many individuals in order to achieve a desired outcome, and reasons why much work is being done on social and political problems with reference to his claim that moral problems are drawing mathematicians and economists to them

Note: Consider the example of Nash Equilibrium mentioned in the introduction - the best outcome is guaranteed by thinking of self-interest as well as the interests of the community - and how it challenged the individual competition of Adam Smith's economic model.

In terms of links with other readings in the anthology, the mark scheme (level 5) suggests you may make reference to Schneewind's initial claims that modern moral dilemmas can no longer be universally solved on a religious basis. Reference to modern ethical concerns, such as abortion or the environment, are likely to be used to support theoretical discussion rather than as a central part of the answer. It seems that this passage, and indeed the wider reading, lends itself to links with ethical theories, such as Kantian deontology and utilitarianism, as well as the views of Hume and Marx.

Pitfalls to avoid:

- Focusing on the whole Schneewind article to the detriment of the selected passage.

- Referring very generally to other ethical theories without relating them to the selected passage.

▸ **(b) Do you agree with the idea(s) expressed? Justify your point of view and discuss its implications for understanding religion and human experience. (20)**

One interesting approach to answering on a passage like this is to "set up your straw man". In other words, state a view and build up critical reasoning about why it is strong or convincing. Then tear it down with your own opinion - based on scholarship and concise, fluent reasoning. You may wish to draw on a wide range of relevant material such as cultural relativism and relevant implications derived from sociology and psychology. Candidates made effective use of topics such as medical ethics, war and peace, environment, animal rights and gender issues.

Implications for religion are wide-ranging here. You need to consider whether religion has a voice at all in ethical considerations, and if so, how loud? There are many interesting contemporary examples to employ here; approaches to social issues such as debt counselling and food banking, being spearheaded by churches; the gay marriage debate; international aid and so on.

For human experience, the mark scheme gives the following advice: candidates are likely to make an increasing number of links between the implications raised about the need for modern ethics to find new approaches to moral philosophy and to consider how successful these have been. They may consider at greater length the implications for society of the "new directions" which modern morality has taken, for example the role of virtue thinking, as well as the acceptance of cultural diversity within moral norms. This may be related to Schneewind's example of the rural retreat. They may consider the implications of key moral issues mentioned, including the preservation of resources and the environment, population control, and the prevention of nuclear war.

Pitfalls to avoid:

- Relying on knowledge from part a, which was not developed into a cohesive argument.

- Scant exploration of implications.

- Not giving an explicit or justified point of view.

- With so many ideas and implications going on, it may be tempting to write with as much breadth as possible, at the expense of academic rigour and analytical depth.

# How to prepare for the examination

## UNIT 3 - DEVELOPMENTS

You need to write answers on **THREE TOPICS**.

You have **1¾ HOURS** in the exam (**35 MINUTES** per question).

You can either complete two questions from Philosophy and one from Ethics, or two from Ethics and one from Philosophy

## *Philosophy of Religion*

You should choose three topics from separate bullet points. Where there is an **OR** you are safe to bank on the regularity of the question. However, where topics share a bullet point, you need to have a strong grasp of the whole bullet point, in order to prepare for a combination question.

- Critiques of Religious Belief, the Argument from Religious Experience and the Ontological Argument

- Life after Death **OR** Religious Language

## Ethics

- Religion and Morality; Deontology, Natural Moral Law, Virtue Ethics

- Ethical Language, meaning and definition of ethical terms with reference to "is/ought" and debates about "good", emotivism **OR** Objectivity, relativism, subjectivism **OR** Justice, law and punishment.

## Making revision notes

The following notes on two selected topics from Philosophy of Religion and Ethics (Unit 3) are helpful for a basic grasp of the main descriptive and evaluative points for each of the topics covered. They are also a guide for how to structure revision notes. As an A-grade student, you will need to add layers of detail from your notes and essays to gain credit in the higher levels, but you can use these pointers as building blocks for well-structured points.

Don't be nervous about substituting scholars or points here for your own ideas: examiners hate trawling through identical material, so use the following as a tool, and make it your own.

# FROM PHILOSOPHY OF RELIGION

## *1 b) The ontological argument*

▸ **Introduction**

- Rational argument - Based on logic, not on sensory experience.

- A priori arguments - Those which rely only on processes of logic to prove a point.

- Deductive reasoning - Where knowledge (or the conclusion) is a logical consequence of the premises.

- "The most intriguing of all the arguments for the existence of God is the ontological argument." (Ian Markham)

▸ **Key scholars - existence (Proslogion 2)**

- **ST ANSELM** - God is that "than which nothing greater can be conceived". To exist "in re" as well as "in intellectu" is superior to existing merely in the mind. Therefore God exists, and the fool says in his heart "There is no God". (Psalm 53:1)

- **DESCARTES** - "Existence can no more be separated from the essence of God than can its having three angles equal to two right angles be separated from the essence of a triangle, or the idea of a mountain from the idea of a valley ..."

- We understand innately God to be the supremely perfect being, with all the perfections as his attributes. Just as a triangle has three sides, so God has existence as part of his essence.

▶ **Critique**

- **GAUNILO** - We cannot bring something into existence just by defining it as a superlative. It would be foolish to say that the "Perfect Island" exists in reality just because we can imagine it.

- **AQUINAS** - Compares the statement "God does not exist" to the statement "truth does not exist". The latter is a contradiction in terms because it denies the assertion it tries to make. In contrast, the former statement can be clearly imagined and is, therefore, not a contradiction in terms.

- **KANT** - Existence is not a predicate because predicates tell us something about the thing we're trying to describe. Existence does not tell us anything about the object we're describing.

▶ **Modern versions - necessary existence**

**NORMAN MALCOLM** (1911-90) rejects Proslogion chapter 2, but builds on Proslogion chapter 3:

- God's existence is either **IMPOSSIBLE**, **POSSIBLE** or **NECESSARY**.

- God's existence is **NOT IMPOSSIBLE**. We can imagine the idea of God's existence without incurring a logical contradiction.

- God's existence cannot be **POSSIBLY TRUE** because only contingent things exist like this

- Therefore, given that God's existence is not impossible, it must be **NECESSARY**.

### ▸ Conclusion

- The first version of the argument is widely understood to have failed, due to Kant's criticism.

- Many object to Malcolm's version because in order for it to be accepted, one must concede that God's existence (necessary) is not the same as other forms of existence (contingent), which is an inaccessible claim for the atheist.

# FROM ETHICS

## 1 a) (iii) Virtue Ethics

▶ **Introduction**

- Different from the other ethical theories in this section - rather than focusing on the actions of a person it considers the question "what kind of person should I be?". In this sense it is often described as a **CHARACTER-BASED APPROACH** to ethics.

- Based on **ARISTOTLE**'s thinking.

- Humans' ultimate goal is flourishing (**EUDAIMONIA**), achieved by developing the characteristics of a virtuous person.

▶ **Key scholars**

- **ARISTOTLE** (384-322 BC): Everything has a telos - a purpose. The right way to act - the Golden Mean will be the balance between two extremes, eg courage is the Golden Mean of cowardice and foolhardiness.

- Virtues are learned/developed over time by practising them and imitating role models, until they become habit. He distinguished between **MORAL** and **INTELLECTUAL** virtues.

- ▸ **Strengths**

  - **ELIZABETH ANSCOMBE** - (Article: Modern Moral Philosophy, 1958) - Ethical codes which lay stress on moral absolutes are anachronistic in a society that has essentially abandoned God, and she urged a return to a morality based on human flourishing. Appeals to both secular and religious people.

  - **ALASTAIR MACINTYRE** (1981) - After Virtue: see Rachels and Vardy.

  - It is practical - Naturalistic theories are overly complex, whilst virtue-based ethics are more applicable to people's everyday lives.

  - What other benefits does the theory have over Kant and NML? You need to compare virtue with these theories as there could be a question on this.

- ▸ **Critique**

  - **KANT** argued that we should do our duty, even when (and especially when) it goes against our natural disposition.

  - **TELEOLOGISTS** - **BENTHAM/MILL/SINGER** would all question the underlying principles of the theory, ie that people should never be used as a means to an end. The theory does not recognise the central importance of consequences.

▸ **Conclusion**

- **VAGUE** - Does the theory provide enough moral guidance in difficult moral dilemmas?

- Does everyone have the time/inclination to pursue the virtues?

- Fails for those who reject cultivation of virtue as the ultimate goal in life.

*I don't know whether there are moral saints. But if there are, I am glad that neither I nor those about whom I care most are among them. - Susan Wolf, Freedom without Reason, 1994*

# Top revision tips - Unit 3

If you are serious about the A grade, prepare well on the less popular topics. Arguably, you will be less likely to repeat the same material as other candidates, and you will have the chance to show off your skills as a philosopher if you write on, for example, atheism or religion and morality.

Make detailed revision plans/cards for each topic selected, making sure you have covered enough areas to guarantee three questions in the examination.

Make vocabulary lists or cards for each of the topics you are studying. Put the key word on one side, and the definition and context on the other. Learn them by reading them through a few times, then using the word as a trigger for the definition. Go for a walk (fresh air helps revision!) and get someone to test you. (Thanks to my mum Diana for doing this for me when I was doing A levels!)

Get hold of as many past question papers as you can from your teacher, or from Edexcel.

Create essay plans using the tips for how to structure question types, found in the "How to analyse past exam questions" section of this book.

- **Practise writing essays under strict exam conditions: 35 minutes (unless you get extra time, then add 25%); no notes; no distractions.**

*It is also worth reiterating that successful candidates are invariably those who have written three complete answers. There is no substitute for timed exam practice well before the event to ensure that candidates are not caught out by poor time management in the exam. - Examiner's Report, 2011*

Swap them with an aspiring A-grader classmate, and mark them, using the examiners' comments on question types included in the above section, as well as the levels descriptors on p119 of the specification (available to download from Edexcel).

Keep doing it, and you will improve and be ready to face any question without surprise or panic!

# Top Revision Tips - Unit 4

Want to be more intelligent? My A level History teacher, Mr Jolly, used to say "the more words you know, the more thoughts you can have". Words are like rooms. Each time you add a new one to your vocabulary, you extend your headspace, and arguably, your intellectual reach.

## KEY WORDS

- Agnostic
- Atheist
- Attribute
- Cognitive
- Empirical
- Fallacious
- Metaphysical
- Necessary
- Phenomena
- Probability
- Proof
- Proposition
- Synthetic
- Transcendent
- Unintelligible
- Verification

Once you have drawn up your list of key words, you could spend some time researching definitions, key ideas and scholars associated with them. Start with a good, regular dictionary, then move to specifically philosophical ones. Some will be longer, more detailed entries (for example, "empirical"). Others will be shorter, (for example, "proposition").

| KEY WORD | DEFINITIONS |
| --- | --- |
| Atheist | *"One who holds the belief that God does not exist" (Concise Oxford Dictionary)*<br><br>*"the negation of theism, the denial of the existence of God" (Stanford.edu website)*<br><br>*Scholars associated: Nietzsche, Sartre, Peter Singer, AC Grayling, JL Mackie, Feuerbach, Bertrand Russell (although see his article "Am I an atheist or an agnostic?" (1947)* |
| Necessary | *"Requiring to be done, achieved; requisite; essential" (Concise Oxford Dictionary)* |

Work through the other readings in the same fashion, making sure that your understanding of the key term in question is "crystal clear".

Make sure your notes contain some original material not covered in class; this is very important to examiners.

Choose some paragraphs at random, (or get a friend to select one for you, and vice versa), and using highlighters and a pen, draw out the key words and phrases and convert into an essay plan.

Using your plan, practise writing answers to past questions under exam conditions, paying strict attention to time limits (1 hour 15 minutes).

Lastly, cultivate a "work hard, rest hard" attitude. A famous missionary once said "wherever you are, be all there". This translates in the modern day into "when you are working, put a note on the door asking not to be interrupted, put your phone on silent and have no social networks or emails pinging at random to disturb you". Likewise, when you are taking a break, don't talk, think or worry about work. Do something that re-energises you like exercise, an episode of a mini-series you love, a hot chocolate with marshmallows ... little treats go a long way.

Lightning Source UK Ltd.
Milton Keynes UK
UKOW05f1938260914

239231UK00001BA/9/P